YALE SCHOOL OF ARCHITECTURE
EDWARD P. BASS DISTINGUISHED VISITING
ARCHITECTURE FELLOWSHIP
LEARNING IN LAS VEGAS CHARLES ATWOOD /
DAVID M. SCHWARZ

Edited by Nina Rappaport, Brook Denison, and Nicholas Hanna

Yale School of Architecture
180 York Street
New Haven, Connecticut 06520
www.architecture.yale.edu

Distributed by
W. W. Norton & Company Inc.
500 Fifth Avenue
New York, New York 10110
www.wwnorton.com

This book was made possible through the Edward P. Bass Distinguished
Visiting Architecture Fellowship fund of the Yale School of Architecture.
It is the fifth in a series of publications of the Bass Fellowship published
through the dean's office.

Edited by Nina Rappaport, Brook Denison, and Nicholas Hanna

Design: mgmt. design, Brooklyn, New York

Cover: Nicholas Hanna

Library of Congress Cataloging-in-Publication Data

Learning in Las Vegas : Charles Atwood / David M. Schwarz / edited by Nina
Rappaport, Brook Denison, and Nicholas Hanna.

 p. cm. — (Edward P. Bass Distinguished Visiting Architecture Fellowship ; 5)

ISBN 978-0-393-73334-1 (pbk.)

1. Resort architecture—Nevada—Las Vegas—History—21st century—Designs
and plans. 2. Architecture—Study and teaching—Connecticut—New Haven. 3.
Las Vegas (Nev.)—Buildings, structures, etc.—Designs and plans. I. Rappaport,
Nina. II. Denison, Brook. III. Hanna, Nicholas.

NA7845.L37L43 2010

725'.804209793135—dc22

2010038002

CONTENTS

Edward P. Bass Distinguished Visiting Architecture Fellowship In 2003, Edward P. Bass, a 1967 graduate of Yale College who studied at the Yale School of Architecture as a member of the class of 1972, endowed this fellowship to bring property developers to the school to lead advanced studios in collaboration with design faculty. Mr. Bass is an environmentalist who sponsored the Biosphere 2 development in Oracle, Arizona, in 1991, and a developer responsible for the ongoing revitalization of the downtown portion of Fort Worth, Texas, where his Sundance Square, which combines restoration with new construction, has transformed a moribund urban core into a vibrant regional center. In all his work, Mr. Bass has been guided by the conviction that architecture is a socially engaged art operating at the intersection of grand visions and everyday realities.

The Bass fellowship ensures that the school curriculum recognizes the role of the property developer as an integral part of the design process. The fellowship brings developers to Yale to work side by side with educators and architecture students in the studio, situating the discussion about architecture in the wider discourse of contemporary practice. In 2005, the first Bass studio, led by Gerald Hines and Louis I. Kahn Visiting Professor Stefan Behnisch was documented in *Poetry, Property, and Place* (2006). The second Bass studio, in 2006, which teamed Stuart Lipton with Saarinen Visiting Professor Richard Rogers ('62), engineer Chris Wise, and architect Malcolm Smith ('97), was documented in *Future-Proofing* (2007). *The Human City* (2008) records the collaboration of Roger Madelin and Bishop Visiting Professor Demetri Porphyrios. *Urban Integration: Bishopsgate Goods Yard* with the Nick Johnson and FAT architecture partnership was collected in 2009. With this fifth book in the series it is a pleasure to present the research and studio led by property developer Charles Atwood and architect David M. Schwarz ('74), Davenport Visiting Professor of Architecture, in *Learning in Las Vegas*.

Preface: Robert A.M. Stern, Dean *Learning in Las Vegas* documents the fifth architect-developer studio to be conducted at Yale, led in fall 2008 by Edward P. Bass Distinguished Visiting Fellow, Charles Atwood who was then at Harrah's Entertainment, and David M. Schwarz, Davenport Visiting Professor of Architecture, who asked advanced students at the Yale School of Architecture to reassess Robert Venturi and Denise Scott Brown's Yale studio of forty years ago and analyze ways in which today's Las Vegas can learn from other places in order to reinvent itself for the future.

Atwood, a graduate of Tulane University with an MBA in finance, joined Harrah's Entertainment Inc. in 1979. He was named chief financial officer in 2001 and became a member of Harrah's board of directors in July 2005. In 2006, he was named its vice chairman. At Harrah's, Atwood oversaw the company's strategic growth initiatives including development, design, and construction through 2009 while also serving on community boards for the Las Vegas Chamber of Commerce and the Las Vegas Performing Arts Center as well as on the Dean's Advisory Board for the University of Nevada-Las Vegas Business School.

David M. Schwarz, who founded his Washington, D.C., and Fort Worth, Texas-based firm in 1978, received his B.A. at St. John's College in Annapolis, Maryland and his master of architecture at Yale in 1974, after which he worked in the office of Paul Rudolph. Committed to a contextual approach, Schwarz regards the past as a repository of ideas that can be adapted to solve modern problems. His projects include the Bass Performance Hall in Fort Worth, the Ballpark at Arlington, and the Environmental Sciences Center Building at Yale, the first Gothic-style building constructed at the university in two generations. In Las Vegas, where this Yale Studio took place, Schwarz has designed the Smith Center for the Performing Arts as a new monumental focus for the city's nascent downtown.

I offer my gratitude to Charles Atwood and David M. Schwarz for their dedication to the studio, as well as to Brook Denison ('07) and Darin Cook ('89), who ably assisted the students in their research and design. I also offer thanks to Nina Rappaport, publications director at the Yale School of Architecture, who with Brook Denison and Nicholas Hanna ('09), one of the students in the studio, co-edited *Learning in Las Vegas*.

Introduction In the forty years since the famous "Learning from Las Vegas" studio led by Robert Venturi and Denise Scott Brown at Yale in 1968, the Las Vegas's Strip has been transformed by explosive growth. The studio's work fascinated developers, planners, architects, gamblers, and entertainers, and the book of the same name became an essential text for both architectural theory and popular culture. The studio asked why the Strip looked the way it did and analyzed its development. Arising from the desert town that boomed with the construction of the Hoover Dam while the rest of the county suffered during the Great Depression, Las Vegas started out as a gaming town in the clutch of the Mafia only to become the escapist resort it is today. But what is this city's future? Charles Atwood, who guided the entertainment company Harrah's in its urban growth strategy, and David M. Schwarz, architect and planner of several Las Vegas projects, collaborated in this new Yale architecture studio, "Learning in Las Vegas." They asked the students to analyze vital urban places around the world and then apply their findings to 270 acres of Harrah's properties located at the center of the Strip.

This book opens with a discussion between Edward P. Bass Distinguished Visiting Architecture Fellow Charles Atwood and Davenport Visiting Professor of Architecture David M. Schwarz about urbanism in Las Vegas in the section titled "Collaborations in Design and Development." The next section, "Teaching in Las Vegas," includes an essay on the Strip by Mr. Schwarz, a selection of photographs from the original 1968 Las Vegas studio paired with those taken by the 2008 Yale students, the essay "Imagineered Worlds" by geographers Steven Flusty and Paulina Raento, discussions with public officials and developers, and the students' analyses of Harrah's site—all of which provide insight into the social and physical development of the Las Vegas Strip and its relationship to the broader cityscape. The following section, "Learning in Las Vegas," begins with the students' analyses of successful urban environments around the world, continues with the students' master-plan designs and their specific resort designs, and concludes with excerpts from the discussion that accompanied the final review of the student's work.

Throughout the research, analysis, and design phases, students absorbed the culture of Las Vegas while visiting and analyzing other cities for inspiration. To understand how the city works and how it differs from other cities, the students met with Las Vegas developers and officials, including Las Vegas Mayor Oscar Goodman; Gary Loveman, chairman, C.E.O., and president of Harrah's; visionary urban developers Craig Robbins in Miami and Henry Miller in Dallas; and Alan Feldman, a senior vice president with MGM. Financial experts weighed in on developers' goals and expectations, giving the students context and cautionary advice. While the studio was in session, financial markets collapsed, which altered assumptions about development on the Strip and heightened the student's sensitivity to the economics of design.

Having studied the urban planning behind successful cities, the students applied strategies to their own projects. By midterm, in teams of two, they completed their analysis and master plans, which were then used as a basis for specific individual resort designs. The project descriptions close the book along with the final-review jury participation of developers Edward P. Bass, David Bonderman, Alan M. Feldman, Robert B. Frey, Greg Miller, Marc Rowan, Brian Yost, and Richard Fields, and architects Deborah Berke, Leon Krier, and Keller Easterling.

The editors would like to acknowledge the work of the students (all class of 2009) who participated in the studio and whose cooperation was essential to this book: Terry Chew, Cheng-Hui Chua, Nicholas Hanna, Eric Krancevic, Louise Levi, Patrick McGowan, Lauren Mishkind, Zakery Snider, Christopher Starkey, and Tom Tang. We also extend our appreciation to the work of copy editor David Delp and graphic designer Sarah Gephart of mgmt. design, New York.

I. COLLATIONS IN DESIGN DEVELO

BORA-

I

AND

PMENT

Developer / Architect Charles (Chuck) Atwood and David M. Schwarz discuss the role of the developer and architect in building mega resorts as well as strategies to urbanize Las Vegas.

Nina Rappaport Charles, as Harrah's financial director and vice chairman, how did you become involved in real estate development, and what is your role with the company regarding in new mixed-use development in Las Vegas?

Charles Atwood I was first involved with large, mixed-use developments in New Orleans, where I went to school and worked for ten years. I have worked for Harrah's on a number of real estate developments for nearly thirty years. As vice chairman, I am in charge of our new development and design and construction. What we are doing in Las Vegas is unusual in our industry. Historically, buildings in Las Vegas were fortresses; once guests were inside, they were not intended to go out. This contradicts demonstrated consumer behavior—people want to have a fun entertainment experience, including visiting an average of 5.5 resorts each day. We now have acquired enough facilities and land to make it not only possible but desirable for customers to move from place to place. This new vision requires a more expansive approach to Las Vegas as to how real estate is organized. The 350 acres of contiguous land Harrah's owns is prime real estate located at the heart of Las Vegas' world-famous Strip. With nine resorts and more than 20,000 hotel rooms already in place, the objective of the development is to add new attractions while at the same time ensuring the contiguous resort's interstitial space seamlessly connects the properties.

NR Has the attitude changed now that the commercial and entertainment industries in Las Vegas have become more involved in urban planning issues? How do you fit the Harrah's complex into the urban design of Las Vegas and incorporate your concepts into creating a city?

CA I would say Las Vegas is growing up. It is now being developed around modes of transportation other than just the automobile. Historically, the major highway, the Las Vegas Strip, was for automobiles and not very friendly to pedestrians. Over time that roadway system became insufficient to carry all the traffic. Now there is another "road-way" to move people from place to place, the Las Vegas monorail. It is interesting because we can have architecture on both sides of the highway and both sides of the monorail. Now that we have a mass-transit system, it is possible for people to abandon the automobile. Further, the pedestrian experience can be much more vibrant as buildings are linked together in a number of places—all this is urbanization, in my view.

David M. Schwarz Architects

Nancy Lee and Perry R. Bass Performance Hall,
Fort Worth, TX, 1996

David M. Schwarz Architects

Nancy Lee and Perry R. Bass Performance Hall,
Fort Worth, TX, 1996

NR I see this as similar to the tendency to cluster various venues related to the same commercial urban condition—for instance, the way gallery districts develop in cities such as New York.

CA For us, it is all about guest experience; what makes our development unusual is that we want to encourage people to enjoy a wide variety of experiences. One place might have a set of experiences designed around a particular demographic group, but those same people might also enjoy experiences with other demographic groups. That would never have happened ten years ago; guests would not have been encouraged to mingle and move about. Today the city is more enlightened about how people use entertainment spaces, so now we are making it easier to move around.

NR David, how do you see Las Vegas from an architect's perspective? Do you also feel it is in a new phase that recalibrates what is there and revises former mistakes?

David Schwarz One of the interesting things about Las Vegas is that there is a desire among very diverse communities to have a "real city." The impetus is a broad-based desire for Las Vegas residents to look outside their borders and to understand urbanism. How do you create a neighborhood? Across all sectors of Las Vegas there is a desire to grow up. Harrah's is choosing to capitalize on this desire to become an authentic place.

NR Chuck, how do you engage architects and urban designers in this process? Do you initiate proposals? Do you have your own vision, or do you look to architects and designers for advice?

CA I have a performance strategy and a specific idea of how the land should be used. The vision is to have people move from place to place within our neighborhood and make The Strip, specifically the corner of the Las Vegas Strip at Flamingo Road, the center of activity for the city. Taken together, the buildings constitute an iconic place. If you saw a picture of it you would immediately know it was Las Vegas. We have engaged a wide variety of people from around the world to create just such an environment—"the place" in Las Vegas. It is the equivalent of the Spanish Steps in Rome, Piccadilly Circus in London, and Red Square in Moscow. We've looked at a wide array of alternatives and are narrowing that array to a plan that is iconic, guest-friendly, environmentally appropriate, and, importantly, affordable.

NR Whom did you bring in to assist the process?

CA In addition to David Schwarz, James Cameron, the film director, helped with some very interesting things, putting technology and entertainment together with architecture. We also consulted with Civic Arts/Eric Kuhne (London) on the overall plan. Hettema Design (Pasadena) focused on developing a relevant "place" for Gen X. Priestman Goode (London) is working on a renovation of Imperial Palace, and 360 Design (Kansas City), HOK Sports (Kansas City), and Make Architects (London) are working on an arena. We work with many people and firms, including a number of local architects and consultants.

NR David, how did you come to know Chuck, and how has your firm worked with developers over its almost thirty years as architects based in Washington, D.C., and Forth Worth, Texas, with many clients in the western U.S.?

DS I met Chuck through my work on the Smith Center for the Arts, in Las Vegas. It comprises four buildings in one city block and demonstrates a new vision for the city. It is far more urban than most of what has been built so far in Las Vegas, and it is located on a vacant 61-acre tract of land the city has master-planned for new, urban development. I was extremely impressed with him as we went through the development process. Chuck was versed in what the performing arts can do for a city and what the physical implications of that are. He is very interested in urban and art issues in the context of the facility. Since the ownership of Harrah's changed hands recently, the company wanted to take a new look, and Chuck was interested in a fresh take. I was lucky enough to be chosen to help. We've done a great deal of planning all over the States. In Texas, for example, we've been studying the issue of pedestrianism for twenty-five years. Our job is to help Harrah's develop an overarching vision of its land and be the guardian of a neighborhood, not just a project. There is a mixed-use pedestrian spine that will connect the Harrah's properties on the Strip to Koval Street and make far more of their land accessible from the Strip. We have done quite a bit of work for Disney with a series of similar problems. I think what is interesting is that Las Vegas is beginning to look at how to be greener, how to impact the environment minimally, and how to be more responsible as well as more sustainable. These are all very good things given our changing times and will create a much more enlightened Las Vegas.

NR What have your relationships with developers and clients been like? When does it work best, and what is a successful project from your perspective?

DS We've always said the best client is the best student. There is never a clear solution to a problem at the outset, so our role is to spend time with our clients to both teach them as well as learn together. We learn how to deal with our clients' needs.

David M. Schwarz Architects

American Airlines Center, Dallas, TX, 2001

We were attracted to Harrah's because we consider our firm to be a populist firm that is less concerned with the architectural critical press than creating places people love. The client is an essential part of the team. The arena in Dallas was a complex endeavor, particularly for the client. How do you create an important civic structure that has the necessary returns? The arena has the highest dollar value of indoor advertising of any arena built to date. How to measure revenue for architecture is a really important issue for people who are in the business. A concert hall is complex: the client wants world recognition and perfect acoustics. How do you give the client something that suits their personality? We learn together.

NR Chuck, how do you see the collaborative process with architects? Do you give them a specific assignment and then leave them alone, or do you work together? And how do you avoid the cookie-cutter development approach in casino design?

CA The process must be collaborative. While we can express how we want it to operate, we need assistance in helping our space come to life as a physical entity. We seek to avoid the cookie-cutter approach by understanding how different people want to use different spaces. Las Vegas has a very strong, already-built context. The physical constraints are strong, and we don't want to repeat the same thing over again, so creative re-use is critical.

NR How do you make a building significant in a city full of iconic buildings? Do you want an iconic building? Does the architectural form matter to you?

CA That is a very interesting question, and it is not just a problem for Las Vegas. The number of developers who want iconic buildings is seemingly endless. There is a very similar feeling to the buildings in Las Vegas. The Las Vegas Strip is what unites these places today. A drive down the Strip will quickly give you a sense of that feeling. We will do something different, which is re-use existing buildings and tie them together with new entertainment spaces. In earlier times a developer would tear down a building to build another designed to be over-the-top. We are determined to take existing buildings and make them as over-the-top as new ones by connecting them with interesting spaces. To do that, we've assembled a team that is sympathetic yet has different visions of the place. What is critically important is to find people with a common vision of the outcome but who still have sufficiently different ways to execute that work so they can produce a place with variety and excitement. We believe to create what feels like an authentic neighborhood requires a diverse set of views. The Las Vegas Strip has been built over time by different people, and we need to authenticate that. The trick to making it accessible is the art of collapsing

Developer / Architect

Harrah's

Caesars Palace Las Vegas

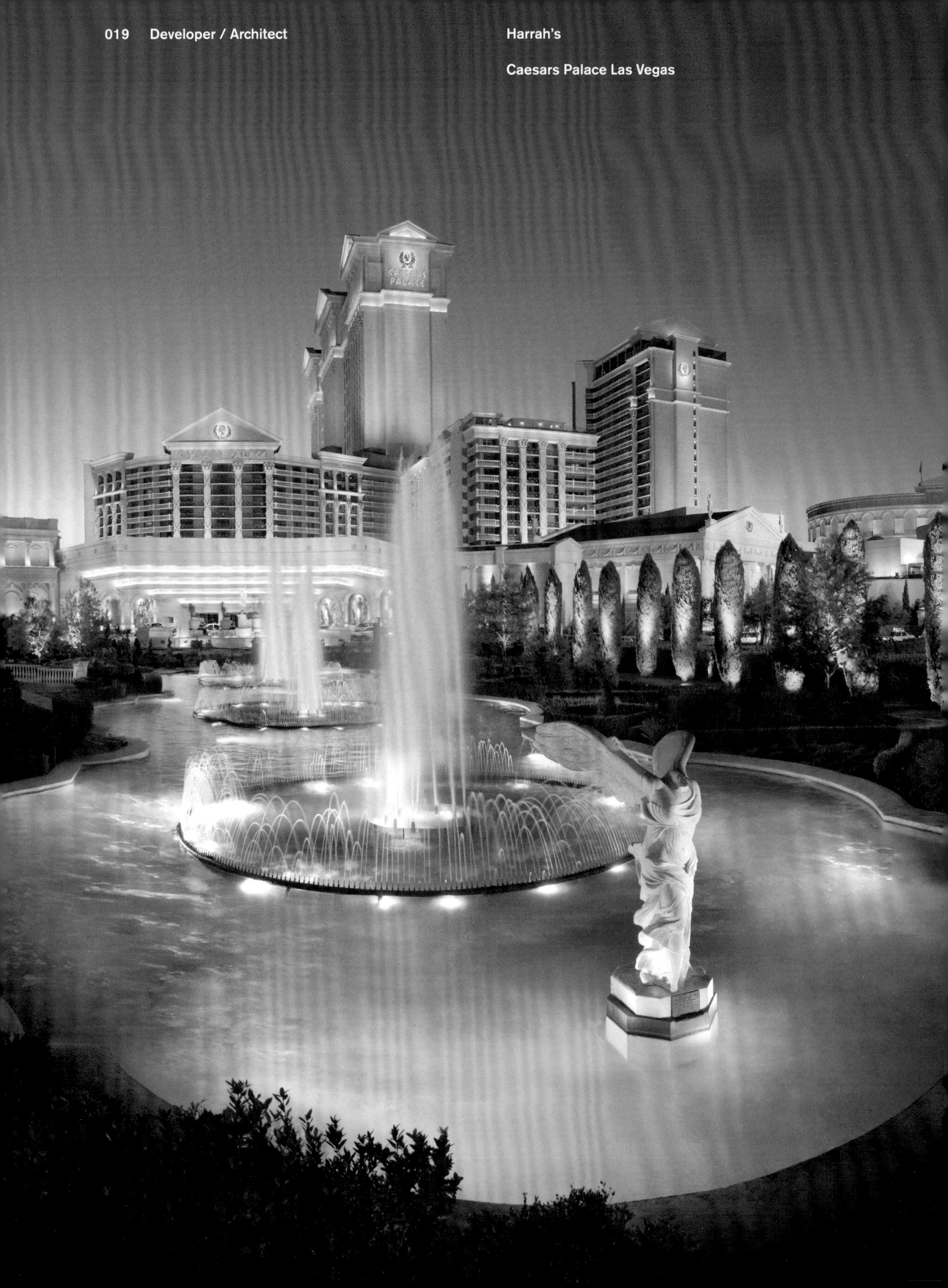

time; we need to create something that feels like it has evolved over time. Our site is 350 acres, and half of it is built out today—how to make it feel like one piece is part of the trick. You have to make people feel like they are in a place that is real and can understand the function of time in the creation of place.

NR How do you build in a desert environment, where there is such a short supply of water? How do you create a comfortable, high-quality building in a hot climate?

DS In Texas, which is like Las Vegas, we tend to focus on the heat, but we should focus on humidity. In Las Vegas it is quite comfortable in the shade. It isn't whether it is hot or cold; it is the time of day. The question then becomes, how do you design so the user follows the flow of the climate? Being able to capitalize on the times when weather is a benefit is quite important.

NR Have you ever worked on a project where something unexpected happened? Have you allowed an element of surprise to come into a project?

CA My talent is on the money side, so virtually every project has unexpected aspects—some good, some not so good. I am always surprised but pleased to see a project built within the budget! We work very hard to be sure we design projects that are viable economically, but we must keep the excitement of the building. One way to accomplish that is to be very clear about project objectives, including target customers, program, and budget, right at the beginning of the project. We have found that talented people can collaborate to create very special places if they understand the problem constraints right from the beginning. Then it simply becomes all about iterating through the process of issue identification and resolution—all while keeping a clear idea of what makes the place special for the guest.

DS Chuck undersells himself. What he is best with is numbers. But I've been most impressed with his insights and how quickly he grasps spatial concepts and how he can talk articulately about them.

NR What is your interest in Las Vegas as the studio's subject? Why now?

DS It is the fortieth anniversary of Denise Scott Brown and Robert Venturi's "Learning from Las Vegas" studio at Yale. It seems appropriate to visit the site now as we have had a great deal of experience from the world at large and are interested in learning how the lessons we've learned in other places are applicable to Las Vegas. The world

has changed significantly, and now entertainment is a part of everything. I first became involved in Las Vegas when Oscar Goodman became mayor, and he just looked at downtown; he was always interested in urban issues. Las Vegas is a city in a very nascent phase of defining itself, internally rather than externally. There is a desire to make Las Vegas a real place since the permanent population is much larger than it was ten years ago. How to make the Strip a more pleasant pedestrian experience is a fascinating question. It is interesting to look at human behavior and see how you take some of that indigenous excitement and instill it in place-making.

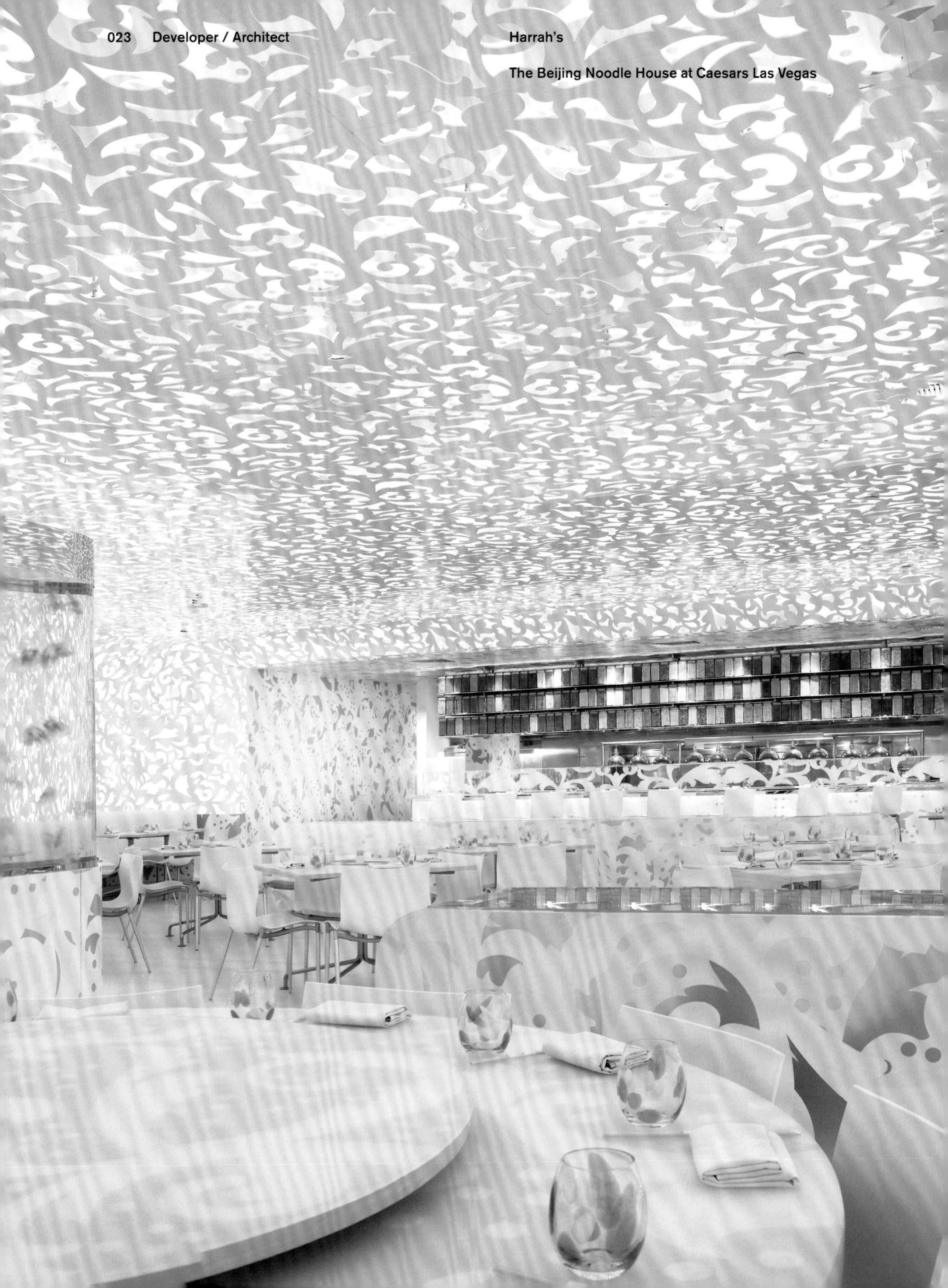

II. TEACH
LAS VEGA
THEN AN

NG IN

AS:

O NOW

ACCESSING LAS VEGAS'S STRIP

David M. Schwarz Las Vegas is one of the most interesting places to study for an architect concerned with patterns of built form, not because it necessarily has paradigms to emulate or embrace but because it is such an intense hub of human activity. While there is nothing that happens in most other American urban centers that does not happen in Las Vegas, what makes up a small fraction of the activity in those cities makes up the majority of what we see and experience on the Strip, which is what makes Las Vegas different.

With their Yale studio "Learning from Las Vegas," Robert Venturi and Denise Scott Brown asked us to reconsider Las Vegas in a new light. At its root, their thesis was a simple one: Las Vegas is a city that came of age in the automobile era, and, as such, a great deal can be learned from studying how those forces created a place that was both special and unique.

But that was forty years ago, and both the world and Las Vegas have moved on. Questions about how we shop, play, and live have multiplied. With their renovation and gentrification, cities are once again desirable places to live. For example, in Washington, D.C., Dupont Circle has become one of the city's most fashionable neighborhoods. In New York City, the meteoric rise in property values has marched continuously from the West Village to the Meatpacking District up through Chelsea and on to Hell's Kitchen, taking a few of Manhattan's worst slums and turning them into some of the city's most expensive real estate. This same pattern has spread across the country to Providence, Rhode Island, Hoboken and Jersey City, New Jersey, Chicago, Miami's South Beach, and on and on. Urban cores have been manufactured in places that formerly lacked them. The New Urbanism movement, spearheaded by Andres Duany, has taken hold for both social and economic reasons that focus on the merit of the traditional American town's form. People like community, and community is supported by urban settings.

During a nationwide movement toward urban dwelling that saw a renewed interest in urban cores, Las Vegas continued to develop according to the same automobile-centric planning model upon which it was founded. It continued to capture the world's imagination with a never-ending game of one-upmanship, each resort outdoing the previous one with bigger and flashier statements. However, it has remained oblivious to the lessons that have been learned across the U.S. For instance, Las Vegas still builds isolated fortresses which, rather than trying to keep the "invaders" out, work very hard to keep their "citizens" in. CityCenter, the most recent fortress, has become a ten-billion-dollar question mark.

The Strip's origins are rooted in accessibility, and its founding establishments were developed as roadside attractions, buffered from the highway by ample parking lots. The message to drivers was clear: pull over, park here, and come in. The earliest operations successfully skimmed motorists from the stream of traffic flowing from Los Angeles to downtown Las Vegas. In time, Strip operations grew, eventually overtaking downtown gaming revenue. As the Strip's volume increased, operators expanded, and the model shifted from roadside convenience to fortress-like entrapment. Once isolated properties expanded outward and bumped into neighbors, designers were inspired to seek architectural solutions that would confuse and sequester casino visitors. One-way moving sidewalks, disorienting interiors, an absence of windows, and abundant, interiorized necessities (food, beverage, and lodging) encouraged visitors to stay as long as possible. The Strip had grown from a handful of highway detours into a boulevard of isolated fiefdoms. Standard infrastructure, like sidewalks and public transportation, were slow to come. Front doors were hundreds of feet from the Strip, and the porte-cochere became the most important and articulated exterior expression.

In 2007, Harrah's Entertainment hired my firm, David M. Schwarz Architects, as their master planner. The company's stated objective was to maximize pedestrian connections between Caesars Palace, the Flamingo, Paris, Harrah's, the Imperial Palace, Bally's, and Planet Hollywood. How has the Las Vegas Strip, in just fifty years, come to this radically different attitude that, rather than discouraging pedestrian life, actively plans for it?

I believe we are at the edge of a new era for the Strip that will see it grow into a place more closely resembling the kind of attitudes that have caused the revitalization of abandoned downtowns of major American cities. Although Las Vegas has remained attractive precisely because it is so different from anywhere else, the once automobile-centric Strip will, for the first time, prioritize pedestrians.

This rethinking of the Strip is happening because it must. To continue supplying the 80,000-plus hotel rooms lining the Strip, efficient means of conveyance—sidewalks connecting resorts in a straightforward (and urban) manner and augmented by pleasant pedestrian environments—must supplement the massive structured parking garages that rely on a fleet of porte-cochere attendants and taxi cabs to keep things flowing smoothly.

Despite the long-standing disparity between Las Vegas' planning and nationwide urban-planning trends, people have always walked in Las Vegas; in fact, they continue to do so in vast numbers and against all odds. Today, every conceivable obstacle has been put in the pedestrian's way: for example, streets that are too wide to comfortably cross, confusing and elaborate bridge systems that baffle users while taking them on a journey much longer than a simple at-grade crosswalk. As evidenced by the 75,000 people passing by the Flamingo daily, people still walk because it is the simplest way to see the Strip, despite the impediments. Further, pedestrianism permits and encour-

The Bellagio seen from the northeast corner of the Strip and Flamingo Road.

The Opera House and Eiffel Tower of Paris, Las Vegas.

Outdoor dining fronting the Opera House façade of Paris, Las Vegas.

ages spontaneous decision-making, a hallmark of the Las Vegas visitor who, unlike other cities' visitors, tends to wander without a destination in mind.

So why have developers employed a different set of rules in Las Vegas? Why did Las Vegas persist in the failed vehicle-friendly and pedestrian-adverse suburban development patterns of the Fifties and Sixties while the rest of the world moved on? More important, should Las Vegas stick to these old paradigms, or should it catch up with the rest of the world by rethinking its attitude toward the pedestrian and the automobile?

The answer to the second question is perhaps easier than the first, and the answer may stem more from necessity than from intellectual or theoretical arguments. Most of the time, the Strip is in gridlock, a fabulous parking lot which, ironically, impedes more often than it facilitates movement. In the absence of good urbanism, the only pleasant way to get from the hotel room to dinner or a show at another resort is to take a taxi because the walk is so exhausting and hot; thus, visitors are forced to drive, though many would prefer walking—if only the environment supported a comfortable walk.

Another aspect supporting pedestrianism on Las Vegas's Strip is the evolution of the ownership structure. In the past, Strip owners built up their business by incremental expansion because they were unable to tap into conventional capital sources: Wall Street wouldn't publicly trade gaming company stock, and traditional lending was out of the question. It took a while for financiers to realize the gaming business is among the more predictable, steady, and profitable sectors of the economy—and that is before the food, entertainment, and booze sales are tallied. Despite outdated tales of free food and drink to lure gamers, Las Vegas today is packed with celebrity chefs. Over the past few years, gaming companies' corporate reports confirm that more than half of a casino's revenue is realized from non-gaming activities. But Wall Street was slow to grasp the potential of the Strip. Caesars Palace's gaming floor is perhaps the best example of Las Vegas's early days of single ownership and incremental growth. Its gaming floor, anchored by the original chandelier pit, spreads out in a serpentine form for hundreds of yards, each expansion seamlessly integrated into the whole. As the gaming floor grew outward, rooms were added upward. Caesars now operates with five towers, one added in each decade beginning with the 1960s (the sixth is built and awaiting an interior fit-out).

From a finance perspective, what should put an end to the single-ownership era is the warming of conventional investors to Las Vegas's impressive balance sheets. For example, by taking on debt, Harrah's Entertainment acquired (rather than developed) seven major resorts at the center of the Strip. Suddenly, resorts that had competed against each other for decades—such as the Flamingo and Caesars Palace—were under the same ownership umbrella, which not only permitted but encouraged the reversal of the defensive formations. Only sixty percent of total gaming revenue is spent in the casino affiliated with the hotel where a visitor stays, which means that forty percent is spent elsewhere. Therefore, it is in ownership's best interest to encourage visitors to move freely from one property to the next, experiencing the kind of brand promiscuity they are inclined to pursue, all the while never leaving the overall owner's campus. This is Harrah's current strategy, and they are not in a unique position: currently, only four companies—MGM, Sands, Wynn, and Harrah's—control almost the entire Strip, and many of their holdings are contiguous. MGM is the largest owner, claiming nearly everything south of Harrah's, and both Sands and Wynn have a pair of adjacent facilities to the north. The perceived utility of barriers has been superseded by annexation; however, old patterns of development continue to persist despite a clear trend of consolidation and annexation.

Pedestrianism is back, and while Las Vegas has yet to absorb and respond to the trend, it cannot resist for much longer. The city's anachronistic attitude toward planning is failing to encourage increased visitorship. Begrudgingly, the Strip will move toward pedestrianism. Meanwhile, people flock to places that are enjoyable to walk. The Third Street Promenade in Santa Monica or Lincoln Road in Miami Beach are just two examples of revitalized urban streets that siphon revenue from stale regional shopping malls. People have become bored with the isolation of the suburban model. Downtown's Main Street is once again popular. People have discovered that they like to walk. This new pedestrianism is not going to kill the mall or the strip center, but those forms are becoming relegated to utility and are no longer places of leisure. Eating and shopping have become entertainment, and a conventional urban fabric featuring pedestrian amenities is the best way to give visitors the mobility and freedom they desire.

After staggering success and growth, the Strip must find efficient ways of meeting visitors' desire to explore. A series of acquisitions and consolidations among owners and operators has laid the groundwork for a philosophical and conceptual realignment. For the first time, owners are starting to encourage pedestrian life on the Strip by planning for flow between properties. As dependency on vehicular access is outstripped by pedestrian activity, people should find an increasingly pleasant and accessible urban environment, facilitating their desire to move from resort to resort. In time, the Strip's development should finally catch up with the rest of the country.

One of the Flamingo's doorless entries.

One of the Flamingo's front doors protruding onto the Strip's sidewalk.

Pedestrians walking north on the Strip past Margaritaville.

TWO STUDIOS

Teaching in Las Vegas In the fall semester of 1968, Robert Venturi and Denise Scott Brown took eleven students to Las Vegas to look at the Strip. In opposition to the Modernist's *tabula rasa* urbanism, they insisted that "there is a way of learning from everything." Their research influenced a generation of architects, and their catchphrases, such as "Main Street is almost alright," came to represent an interest in understanding the development of, as well as working with, the vernacular's materials: billboards, symbols, and streets, including the Strip" typology.

This Bass Fellowship studio, a collaboration between the developer Charles Atwood and the architect David M. Schwarz, was founded on the opposite idea. Forty years after the book *Learning from Las Vegas* focused on the Strip, American cities choke on traffic jams, ugly malls, and burdensome commutes. This studio turned attention away from the later American development patterns and focused on what has been learned elsewhere in the past forty years, suggesting how urban conditions can be applied to Las Vegas' car-based culture. The studio addressed ways to incorporate vital urban characteristics such as mixed-use, high-density buildings, pedestrian-friendly streets, continuous building street frontage, and public transportation.

Since the 1940s, Strip development pioneers like El Rancho Vegas, Frontier and Bugsy Siegel's Flamingo disregarded the restrictive 300-foot by 425-foot grid of downtown Las Vegas, leaving behind the city's zoning oversight and opting for the wide-open expanses found just south of Las Vegas on Highway 91. The development of these fortress-cum-resorts became the standard. Each was fronted by a huge parking lot, and it was impossible to walk from resort to resort. Each resort became an independent world unto itself, and whatever connection between inside and outside one might expect when entering a building was dissolved by the windowless boxes that were filled with fantasy-themed interiors. The Flamingo's low-slung buildings surround a lush tropical pool scene built as a roadside attraction in an otherwise remote desert landscape. Increasingly eye-catching signs attracted drivers from Highway 91, making overtures to passersby with elaborate designs of color and light powered by the abundant and cheap electricity of the nearby Hoover Dam. Development continued in this manner for decades. The signs grew bigger and brighter, the buildings followed, and the themed spectacles housed inside became more and more imaginative. At Caesars Palace, everyone was an emperor. Toga-clad attendants dangled grapevines and offered olive-leaf tiaras to gamblers. Las Vegas came to represent a fantasy world in the middle of nowhere, a place to escape reality.

Despite the scale of growth, the Strip continued to operate and develop much the way it had from its earliest days: visitors arrived by car, parked out front, and disappeared into the resort. Eventually, the roadside Strip model collapsed under the weight of its own success. As the volume of cars and visitors increased, the parking-lot/resort-development model began to saturate, giving way to Band-Aid solutions of free valet parking at the porte-cochere, allowing attendants to move the vehicles ever-farther distances away from the front door without inconveniencing the customer. Back-of-Strip parcels became annexed parking lots, eventually giving way to multilevel garages. New resorts filled in the once-vacant gaps and former parking lots. At some point, it started to work like a city, though without the planning that typically precedes the high-volume traffic. What was once a series of roadside attractions has matured into a dense wall of buildings that define the Strip. This fragmented city fabric suggests a reverse Haussmann effect, one in which the main boulevard developed to the point that it exceeded its capacity. To remedy the situation, urban fabric was brought in to surround the boulevard, augmenting the main artery with numerous small and medium-scale side streets, offering a sense of surprise and delight to pedestrians exploring the idiosyncratic twists and turns. Sidewalks and a regularized street grid began to be inserted, but in many cases it remained irregular or incomplete. Although the Strip is thought of as a continuous arrangement of resorts, each feudal empire applied vastly different attitudes and standards to the pedestrian realm. Some, such as Steve Wynn's Bellagio, which opened in 1998, invested in a comfortable and scenic sidewalk lining the Strip, while other casino operators viewed the sidewalk as the last place they wanted would-be customers to feel comfortable. For the most part, resorts have been slow to reorient themselves to the need for pedestrianism, though anecdotal evidence abounds, usually strictly tied to a revenue model: pedestrian bridges traverse busy corners, seamlessly transforming a sidewalk into a shopping mall. Caesars Palace has attempted to lure passersby through the front door, but the area is still dominated by traffic in the form of a huge porte-cochere, valet parking stands, and a taxi line that can extend to hundreds of feet.

The Yale studio required students to immerse themselves in the culture of Las Vegas so they could then propose a way to intervene. But before they could do that, they had to understand urban design in the rest of the world. At the beginning of the semester they analyzed urban streetscapes and then catalogued specific urban design conditions and elements that they felt contributed to successful streets. From there, midsemester, they worked in teams on a 270-acre design for Harrah's campus and completed the master plan with the insertion of a new building design. Some chose to embrace the madness—or at least try and organize it—by working within the existing resorts, porte-cocheres, and parking lots, while other teams opted to work on undeveloped parcels behind the Strip. Each student team addressed the current and future urbanism of the site by demonstrating an understanding of how it currently functions and by proposing a growth model.

THEN AND NOW

Images from the studio led by Robert Venturi and Denise Scott Brown in Las Vegas.

Roman Soldier, Caesars Palace Hotel and Casino, Las Vegas, 1968.

Images from studio led by David M. Schwarz and Charles
Atwood in Las Vegas.

Roman Figure, Caesars Palace Hotel and Casino,
Las Vegas, 2008.

Venturi and Scott Brown

Stardust Hotel and Casino, Las Vegas, 1968.

Schwarz and Atwood

Flamingo Hotel and Casino, Las Vegas, 2008.

Venturi and Scott Brown

Las Vegas Strip, 1968.

Schwarz and Atwood

Las Vegas Strip, 2008.

Venturi and Scott Brown

Fremont Street neon signs, Las Vegas, 1968.

Schwarz and Atwood

Fremont Street Experience, Las Vegas, 2008.

Venturi and Scott Brown

Thunderbird Hotel and Casino entrance, Las Vegas, 1968.

Schwarz and Atwood

Caesars Palace Hotel and Casino entrance, Las Vegas, 2008

Venturi and Scott Brown

"Tanya" billboard on the Strip, Las Vegas, 1968.

Schwarz and Atwood

Koval Lane, Las Vegas, 2008.

Venturi and Scott Brown

Fremont Street neon signs, Las Vegas, 1968.

Schwarz and Atwood

Fremont Street Experience, Las Vegas, 2008.

Venturi and Scott Brown

Parking lot on the Strip, Las Vegas, 1968.

Schwarz and Atwood

Parking lot behind the Strip, Las Vegas, 2008.

Venturi and Scott Brown

Driving north on the Strip, Las Vegas, 1968.

Schwarz and Atwood

Facing north on the Strip, Las Vegas, 2008.

IMAGINEERED
WORLDS

The Design of Las Vegas Resort-Casinos: Steven Flusty and Pauliina Raento The resort-casinos on the Las Vegas Strip simultaneously induce both excitement and boredom. We explore this contradiction as a by-product of the mega-properties' "scripted" architecture, design, and "imagineered" geographies of displacement. Our focus is upon the concretization of the fantastic and the forced disappearance of messy realities at three scales: the streetscape, the interior design of the resort-casinos, and the micro-environment of gambling. We conclude that the Strip's layers result from the collision of numerous carefully manufactured spatial narratives, written for profit and reliant upon an artful manipulation of geography's basic concepts.

—*Profit can be hidden behind entertainment, and power can be hidden behind dullness.*[1]

We *like* Las Vegas. It is a dream place for a geographer's time out. Whatever is new on the Strip stimulates talk about the gaming industry, urban development, design and architecture, and the manipulation of space and time for profit and entertainment. Geography is so much *fun,* we conclude, and then eat, drink, gamble, and shop some more.

And then we drop. A kind of anxiously overstimulated boredom quickly sets in. Academic analysis devolves into wryly imagining parodic resort-casinos. We create a Soviet-themed *Moscow Nights,* where the buffet is consistently understocked, the service is wretched, and guests review an automated hourly May Day parade from atop a half-sized Lenin's Tomb. Our favorite attraction becomes the escalators to the Strip's pedestrian overpasses, which cost nothing to ride again and again. The signage that declares the sidewalks protest-free zones becomes more interesting than the flashy electronic billboards. Most disturbingly, from the casinos' perspective anyway, we start neglecting to gamble.

We find ourselves willfully misreading the Strip. But the problem of subversively (mis)misreading the Strip (at least from the gaming industry's viewpoint) is clearly not limited to us, a couple of wiseacre geographers. The casino's clientele seems to drop as many sardonic comments as they do quarters, and the frequency with which Las Vegas visitors, after a few days' exposure, will refer to the place as both "exciting" and "boring" in the same breath is startling.

How can a place be so exciting and boring *simultaneously*? This seemingly blatant contradiction, we suggest, is not in the statement itself, but in the disjuncture between the resort-casino's explicit and implicit messages and in the ways they are delivered.

Reading the Strip

The contemporary Las Vegas resort-casinos are prime examples of "scripted spaces"—places that are designed as narratives.[2] Like good stories, casinos "have their erotics: tantalization, hunger, a certain withholding, a being teased close, a wait, the lure of even greater pleasure."[3] The audience of these stories participates actively in the stories unfolding as the spaces invite the audience to explore. This exploration appears as a fantastic journey that transports the reader to someplace else, away from the everyday.

Since the early 1990s, the mega-sized resort-casinos on Las Vegas Boulevard, or the Strip, have sought to create a holistic entertainment experience for visitors, who then consume to the benefit of the gaming enterprise. The careful manipulation of space and time is hidden behind the consuming individuals' "freedom to invent their own story" and their "happy imprisonment" in the experience.[4] The prime tools for this manipulation are architecture, design, and gaming's sophisticated relationship with entertainment.[5] These elements underscore the role of geography in the creation of themed environments: the resort-casinos invoke romantic and mythical places, places of cultural finesse and power, and places of action, excitement, and fantasy.[6] Arguably, the resort-casinos and this philosophy have taken the Strip beyond mere theming by giving Las Vegas yet another landscape, another sense of place, and another species of visitors.

But the same mechanisms that induce the underlying suspension of disbelief can be read more critically or, perhaps, cynically. In literary criticism it is now commonplace to assume that texts are produced by not only their author, but more so in their reception by the reader.[7] Following this line of reasoning, if Las Vegas resort-casinos are manipulatively scripted spaces, fantastic and even escapist architectonic narratives for sale, to what extent might the customers' versions of the story diverge from those plotted out by the casino, generating counternarratives subversive to the designer's, manager's, and financier's authorial intent? This question is important. With a storybook, divergent readings are part of the fun. Once the book is purchased, the reader is free to reconstruct the text as divergently as the imagination allows, with the narrative subsequently enriched at no loss to the publisher. But if the resort-casino is a book, then it is a book one pays to read by the chapter (or even by the word). With no predetermined length or final page, one can go on reading as long as one's bank balance permits. In fact, the resort-casino's real purpose is to sell a story and to keep on selling it, rather than just to tell it. Continuing with the literary metaphor, the production cost of the resort-casino "text" exacerbates this pay-as-you-read dynamic. A storybook hardly costs over two billion dollars to publish and entails far less fiscal suffering should it land on the discount rack.[8] In short, the resort-casino cannot afford to have its narrative read *too* creatively, because it may harm revenue. It is thus faced with the task of framing its ongoing story so as to minimize the risk of divergent, critical readings.

This problematic is magnified for the larger spatial script of the entire Strip. If each resort-casino is a scripted spatial story, then the Strip is an anthology rather haphazardly edited together by the invisible hand of the leisure market. So, what strategies would preclude subversive readings—and their corollary obstacles to lightening visitors' pockets—along the length of an urbanesque boulevard? How can the stories that comprise any real city, like Las Vegas as a whole, be edited out—the story of the new immigrant sidewalk leafleteer or that of the labor organizer outside the open-shop casino?[9]

The Strip and its constituent resort-casinos are thus faced with a conundrum answerable only with dissimulation raised to the level of the *Gesammtkunstwerk:* the need to write large a grand narrative proclaiming "What you want, when you want," predicated upon an iron-clad subtext more akin to the highwayman's "Stand and deliver!"[10] Of course, these two proclamations are blatantly contradictory. It would require some prodigiously suspended disbelief to prevent a subtext so mercenarily regimented from plainly showing through. And it is precisely this suspension of disbelief that is secured by means of the tight and thorough theming of the Strip's resort-casino environments.

We examine the Strip's contemporary architecture, design, and geographies at three different scales. The first is the view from the outside: the landscape, people, and buildings of the Strip. The second looks at the inside: the interior design of the gaming properties. The third scale is the micro-environment of gambling.

Brazen New World
The resort development on the Strip—on Highway 91, which stretches from downtown Las Vegas toward Los Angeles—began in the early 1940s. The property that transformed Las Vegas "into a full-fledged resort city" was the Flamingo Hotel, opened in 1946. Gangster Bugsy Siegel's creation took Las Vegas casinos beyond their western heritage by combining "the sophisticated ambiance of a Monte Carlo casino with the exotic luxury of a Miami Beach–Caribbean resort."[11] It mixed fantasy with the recreational experience of its Angeleno clients, anchoring Las Vegas firmly to the growing market in Southern California.[12]

The first consistently themed property on the Strip was Caesars Palace, opened in 1966. This "Greco-Roman palace in the desert" was the most expensive of its era. The property featured oval motifs carved out of imported

1. *The Mirage,* a milestone of the mega-resort-casino boom since 1989, with a tropical theme beginning at curbside.
2. *Paris,* Las Vegas, with its half-sized Eiffel Tower helpfully flagged to assure visitors they have not inadvertently tres-passed upon the European Union.

Italian marble, Romanesque statues, and fountains.[13] The theme was complete with the appropriate naming of the property's segments.[14] For example, the hottest names in show business performed at the Circus Maximus, an 800-seat theater resembling ancient Rome's Flavian Amphitheater—the Colosseum.[15] The development coincided with the growing importance of themed environments and entertainment in American recreation (Disneyland had opened in 1955).[16]

Still, most Las Vegas casinos were strictly about gambling. Little, if any, attention was paid to the design of these spaces, and many operators considered any detour from the games harmful to revenue.[17] Low ceilings, dimmed lights, poor signage, and tightly packed casino floors in warehouse-like settings were meant to keep the customer focused on the game.

The Mirage changed all this in 1989. The $620-million resort was the first property to be built on the Strip for sixteen years. The Y-shaped complex of three gold-and-white towers had thirty stories and more than three thousand hotel rooms (figure 1). In the front, a lagoon surrounded a volcano that erupted every fifteen minutes after dark. A moving walkway transported the visitors from the street into a tropical fantasy world impregnated with attractions and enter-tainment options. "It was like stepping through a green looking glass into a realm of make-believe," and something Las Vegas had not yet seen. [18] The interior space was creative, elegant, luxurious, intimate but roomy, and carefully detailed to maintain the theme and an evoked sense of place throughout the property. It was the first true example of a resort-casino "where the idea was to generate income" instead of minimizing expenses—"and the hell with the cost."[19] In the words of The Mirage's visionary developer Steve Wynn, "It's what God would've done, if He'd had the money."[20]

The result had profound implications for the rest of the gaming industry. Soon after The Mirage's opening, most of the principal corporations were rebuilding for the forthcoming decade, and entirely new projects were planned. This development marked a dramatic change in scale, for the new resort-casinos were larger in size than any of their predecessors, and they were built rapidly from scratch, instead of being piecemeal extensions of existing entities. Each had tens of thousands of square feet of gambling space and several thousand rooms. By the end of 1999, Las Vegas had over 120,000 hotel rooms, most of them on the Strip. Almost 30,000 more had been built by the end of 2009.[21]

The mega-properties are consistently themed, drawing from world geography, history, and fantasy (figure 2). Their philosophy is to make leaving and going elsewhere difficult by emphasizing non-gaming amenities that include shopping, dining, "world-class" entertainment, spas, sports facilities, and art collections. Many properties have state-of-the-art convention facilities, making Las Vegas one of the leading convention destinations in the country.[22] Attracting a diverse customer base is necessary in a context of cutthroat competition that is increasingly global. The customers are more demanding because they can choose from several destinations. Image, identity, and other markers of distinction have gained importance in the saturating market—after all, the games and the odds are virtually the same everywhere.

With this upscaling, the image of the entire city changed from kitsch and glitz toward elegance and quality. More people travel to Las Vegas each year. About half of them come from the American West and about a quarter from Southern California. The visitors are better educated and more affluent, and they spend more. The city attracted over 36 million visitors in 2009—up from 21 million in 1991 and from 34 million in 1999. A typical visitor is a white, married, middle-aged urbanite who is on vacation and traveling with another adult. Forty-seven percent have finished college (32 percent in 1991 and 39 percent in 1999), and 38 percent have a household income of $80,000 or more (11 percent in 1991 and 22 percent in 1999).[23] They stay for an average of 4.6 days (3.9 in 1991 and 4.7 in 1999), and nine out of ten go home "very satisfied."[24]

Las Vegas made $8.8 billion in gaming revenue in 2009; of that total, the Strip made $5.6 billion. This revenue increased steadily through the 1990s, had its ups and downs in the 2000s, and reached an all-time high of $10.9 billion in 2007.[25] Of total revenue, gambling revenue generated by the Strip properties has decreased because there is so much to do, fewer people gamble, and the average gambling budget has declined in relative terms. Eighty-three percent of visitors to Las Vegas gambled in 2009 (down from 90 percent in 1991), with an average budget of $481 ($431 in 1991, and $560 in 1999).[26] In contrast, more money was spent on food, drink, shopping, and entertainment. Most striking, the cheap buffet heaven has become a place for upscale dining: those who spent money on food and drink during their stay paid $250 in 2009, compared with merely $27 in 1991 and $173 in 1999.[27] The declining share of gambling in the overall budget reflected the new Las Vegas customer, who "is a traveling consumer of entertainment who happens to gamble" and is willing to pay for this experience.[28] Furthermore, the clientele became more international. The proportion of foreign visitors reached an all-time record of 19 percent in 1997. It then declined to resemble foreign visitation in the early 1990s, which was at 11 percent of all visitors in 1999 and 14 percent in 2009.[29]

3. Signage along the Strip is integral to the architecture, simultaneously identifying, branding and theming the properties.

4a. The dome of the Great Mosque of Córdoba, at *The Aladdin. 1001 Nights* provided both a luxuriantly vertical space and, subsequently, a topically problematic theme.

4b. Constant Transformation. Planet Hollywood's reconquista of *The Aladdin* retains the verticality but with considerably reduced opulence.

Curb Appeal: The City as a Sign

New York–New York, "The Greatest City in Las Vegas™," is a New York City–themed property on the southern end of the Strip at the corner of Tropicana Boulevard. A roller coaster criss-crosses the most important landmarks of the famous world city, completed in 1997 with a Statue of Liberty, Empire State and Chrysler buildings, a Brooklyn Bridge, a Grand Central Terminal, 2,024 hotel rooms, and an 84,000-square-foot casino.[30] "That's the same Pepsi-Cola sign that is in New York!" observes a lady who has stopped to take a closer look. She wants to go in, but her husband is determined to start with Paris. "We've been in New York. Let's go to Europe."

New York–New York, Paris, and the other "cities" in Las Vegas are prime examples of narrative spaces that transport the visitor to someplace else. Like in good stories, the events "must be spatially anchored" in order to evoke a credible sensation of a journey[31]—no wonder that many of the new resort-casinos have roller coasters or sophisticated fantasy-ride simulators.

These cities in Las Vegas also testify to the dramatic redefinition of signage in casino design during the past few decades. As in the literary world, the appearance of the suggested story—the title and cover of the book—are crucial in the decision to purchase and read the book.[32] The signs on the Strip still identify and inform, but they have also become integral components of a property's overall theme (figure 3). Reflecting the expanded importance of information technology in resort-casino design, "giant message centers" have replaced many of the flashy neon signs for which Las Vegas used to be so famous.[33] These massive towers of the "Electronic Baroque" era combine electronic billboards, sound and light effects, movement, live videos, and sophisticated computer graphics to attract attention and portray an image.[34] The entire building is a central part of this advertisement task. In the words of a sign designer, "Instead of putting a sign up on the wall, the wall and the sign become one."[35]

This union of signage and architecture conveys the property's theme and sets a tone that reflects the atmosphere inside. It also ensures a deeply immersive, experientially convincing, and hence an imposed and tightly controlled narrative theme. This is critical as visitors become smarter about, and more critically suspicious of, simulated environments. A "decorated shed"—borrowing *Learning from Las Vegas* terminology—is no longer sufficient: it feels all too thin and hollow, and leaves too much room for reinterpretation.[36] Instead, the building must look, walk, quack, smell, and feel like a "duck" if the visitor is to be engaged and held in place, undissenting. In the process, the whole gives an identity to the property and distinguishes it from competitors. The imperatives of product differentiation reign

5. Distance and Curb Appeal. Intimately adjacent in their insularity, resort-casinos cluster along the Strip, beckoning customers with curbside attractions (note The Mirage's volcano in mid-eruption at the lower left).

supreme here, for a unique appearance is crucial to seducing people off the street and into the casino: "The one that catches your eye is the one you want to go to."[37]

Many of the resort-casinos on the Strip are cleverly designed as "cities," as busy hubs of contact, exchange, and exploration. Cities are exciting. By promising visitors "anything and everything" they might desire, cities are self-sufficient.[38] They are also "Open 24 Hours," as one Las Vegas advertisement campaign proclaims. It makes sense then that the new CityCenter development prominently features the work of some half-dozen "starchitects," effectively theming the massive complex after idealized elite visions of the world city.[39] Nor is it accidental that established visions of European cities have predominated in recent theming, conveying an upscale sense of pedigreed cultural cache for the American mind. A cruise along the Strip thus becomes an illusionary grand tour of the Continent. For many, this powerful illusion of a journey is more fun than its real counterpart, which requires dealing with passports, jet lag, and strange people and languages. Smooth, convenient, and yet exotic and bizarre, it offers a taste of difference without the necessity of negotiating potentially unsettling characteristics of international travel.[40] The continental vacation in Las Vegas is thus less European than "Pseuropean."[41]

By replicating the world's most important centers of power, wealth, and cultural capital, Las Vegas has assembled the world in one place and topped it with opportunities to travel in time.[42] Worlds both past and present are within walking distance in Las Vegas: New York–New York is almost across the street from Paris and next to tropical jungles, ancient Egypt, Arthurian England, Italies of different eras, and the mythical deserts of Araby (although that last, in keeping with the Strip's constant transformation, has been slowly "terraformed" into Planet Hollywood [figures 4a and 4b] since mid-2003). This overcoming of distance is far from what the Strip used to do. As its nickname suggests, Las Vegas Boulevard used to be a very linear and car-dependent space.[43] It was also compartmentalized and insular, as the crowds concentrated inside casinos, which were considerably distant from one another.

The era of mega-resort architecture and growth have significantly reduced this insularity. There are now more structures on the Strip, and they have a unique "curb appeal" (figure 5). As a result, more people mill around "in no particular direction," transforming the street into "non-directed space—and a place."[44] Indeed, the Strip's unique concentration of collaged architectural fantasies, divergent pre-recorded soundscapes, dancing waters, explosions, animated signage, and omnipresent glare from the electronic billboards is ideally suited to inducing a disoriented fascination in passersby. In malls, this phenomenon is known as "the Gruen Transfer," or "the moment when a 'destination buyer,' with a specific purchase in mind, is transformed into an impulse shopper, a crucial point immediately

6. Obstructions to Obstruction. The Strip is a gray area
of public and private jurisdictions in which rights to free
expression are commonly rendered secondary to the interests of resort-casino corporations.

visible in the shift from a determined stride to an erratic and meandering gait."[45] On the Strip, the Gruen Transfer is
brought into play on a heretofore unheard-of scale, dazing and bemusing city-blocks full of pedestrians. And dazed
and bemused wanderers are more readily fleeced wanderers.

Less cynically, in a contemporary American society in which public space (or space used as such) has been shrink-
ing drastically, mingling with the crowd is *fun*.[46] For the resort-casinos, every driver is a potential pedestrian. The
architectures serve to seduce them out of their vehicles: "Try to drive down Las Vegas Boulevard—it's virtually grid-
locked, so there has to be some entertainment value to it. With just the size and number of signs and lightbulbs—
people just stand there in awe."[47] In order to enhance this experience and provide convenient access, Las Vegas has
made walking easier. The casinos can be reached via escalators and free trams that separate the pedestrians from
the congested traffic on the boulevard. This strategy is a clever way to control the crowd: often the only way from the
tram stop to the street goes through the casino, and the connecting walkway can be reached only by stepping inside
the property's shopping area. But generally, the sidewalks are wide, and there is plenty to see. Or, more precisely,
there is plenty of the *right* things to see, with as few counternarratives in sight as possible. For example, those parts
of the Strip's sidewalks that are public rather than casino property, and the pedestrian bridges across the Strip, have
been largely purged of the threat of visible labor dissent and the inconvenience of the sex industry's leafleteers
through the posting of signs forbidding "obstructive uses" (figure 6). In a place marketed with claims of "anything
goes," "anything" does not include the public exercise of political free speech or the touting of sexual services.

Bringing In the Outside
Once the customers step inside the property, the goal is to keep them there. The longer they stay, the more they
spend. The success of this seduction depends on credibility, on fulfilling the spectacular promise made outside. The
space should therefore unfold like any good story: it should surprise, entertain, flow effortlessly, and let the reader
identify with the hero. A good story lets its reader's imagination fly free, and excites with curiosity-provoking details,
adventure, and romance.[48]

But nothing in this journey is random or accidental, despite the illusion of freedom. The philosophy of contemporary
resort-casino design is to make "all the components work together" so that "[e]verywhere you turn, you're reinforced
by the theme of the property."[49] "[T]he most mature variations of special effects in the world" are employed in the
task.[50] Lights, sounds, and rotating signs and statues are used to direct attention, enhance the atmosphere, and
stimulate. Colors, odors, and carpet designs connect to specific moods and create powerful associations.[51] The

7. Sign-posting lamp post, Paris, Las Vegas. An archetypal compendium of "streetmosphere," with facilities pointed out in readily comprehensible French. Note also the Art Nouveau floral stanchion concealing the observation camera at the lower left, the platform-style "mini-roofs" above the gaming area, and the artificial sky concealing the ceiling overhead.

8. Thresholds, axes, and centerpieces, including Dale Chihuly's flowers, in an independent attraction inside the lobby at the Bellagio.

signage includes written indicators, pathways printed on the carpets, video screens, signposts, and sculptures that draw attention with light, sound, and movement. The purpose is to guide and encourage, not to confuse or intimidate (figure 7). Plants, rocks, moving water, and other elements of nature enhance the sense of illusion and fantasy. This enrichment is particularly powerful in Las Vegas due to its distance from the city's arid reality and the man-made commercialism of the resort-casino. Identifiable elements also enhance the legibility of the space—or, less euphemistically, enforce the casino corporation's authoritative narrative—by providing order and a sense of safety, even if the marked route's meandering typically adds to one's mileage.[52]

The space itself is important in the resort-casino. Small spaces "create the illusion that the casino is busy, even when it's not."[53] Closed spaces offer protection and—especially in the case of high-stakes gambling—privacy, exclusivity, and, not incidentally, surveillability. Corners, nooks, and centerpieces are intimate and orderly, and invite exploration by offering variety.[54] Vertical and wide spaces, such as open ceilings and broad aisles, dissolve congestion and create a sense of roominess, often associated with wealth and elegance. Creative use of space also adapts to a variety of needs. In the words of one designer, "doubling the size of the aisles" accommodates "wheelchairs and walkers" in those properties where the patrons are elderly.[55] Happy customers mean more money.

Luxurious lobbies, one product of the emphasis on non-gaming spaces, rapidly evolved into important focal points that impress and accommodate the consumer. The lobby "sets the tone of the resort and helps distinguish the property."[56] Instead of dragging their luggage through the casino, the clients use a separate entrance that is "never far from the action, yet [the clients] are not inundated" by the casino's congestion.[57] This separation offers a threshold, a center, and an axis, all central in creating "a clear sense of arrival" that is "welcoming" (figure 8).[58]

The Mirage was the first Las Vegas property to sacrifice prime gambling space for a lobby that makes the customers feel they are arriving in style. The property's lobby is an independent destination within the resort. The tropical theme is everywhere. A 20,000-gallon saltwater aquarium fills the wall behind the reception desk. The sharks, the advertised celebrities among the tropical fauna, "can be seen swimming side by side with eels, sea bass, and puffer fish" and attract patrons to have their picture taken in front of the fish tank.[59] The thick carpet under the visitors' feet is decorated with colorful circles of fruit and flowers with a contrasting dark background. The lampshades repeat the flower theme; the lights are dimmed—the evening is just about to set in the jungle. The counters and other structures are made of natural materials or, in the finest tradition of *faux,* at least appear to have been made of stone and wood. The air smells of coconut. An illuminated map of the property anchors this tropical geography in the Caribbean

9. Central Park, New York–New York, Las Vegas.
Reconstructions of nature and miniature streetscape simu-
late inside the outside.

through naming: the convention and meeting areas include rooms named for Antigua, Barbados, Bermuda, Jamaica, and Trinidad.[60] This attention to detail is a crucial element in keeping customers attentive and involved: "In details is credibility established, authenticity verified, trust secured. Mistakes in detail can render a [story] unacceptable."[61]

A tropical "garden alley" connects the lobby to the casino. This corridor is a lush, pleasant passage that invites its explorer farther into the space. It is a prime example of the general trend in interior design of bringing "the natural" indoors, especially since the mid-1980s (figure 9). The explorer is wrapped in an abundance of trees, plants, and foliage that surround a waterfall and little streams. Some of the plants are real, but it is hard to tell which ones. The *faux* vegetation is replicated or preserved through complex and expensive freeze-drying processes to look and feel "as botanically correct as possible."[62] Other sensory elements, such as smell, sound, and fog, support the visual elements and further distance the experience from the surrounding desert. A clever detail confusing the visitor's sense of authenticity, a small sign casually embedded in this "environscape," resembles those displayed in botanic gardens and states a plant's common and scientific names as well as its geographical origin. The detail also entertains by provoking curiosity.

Yet, another detail breaks the narrative's credibility and opens the door to misreading: the soundscape that deviates from the rhythm of the overall space. Instead of Caribbean or Latin sounds, or even crickets and exotic birds, soft mainstream pop music plays in the background and feels grossly *out of place,* undermining the suspension of disbelief.

Nevertheless, a surprise awaits the explorer in the end, like in a good story. The bustling casino—"where the operator would prefer the patron to be"[63]—appears as a busy village at journey's end. Particularly clever is that each section of this vast space has "a sense of intimacy, of its own locale."[64] It has been broken down into a humane, people-friendly scale, "into small, non-threatening, explorative areas" that are clearly legible as soon as the visitor crosses the threshold between the green alley and the casino "village."[65] In addition to gambling, the customer can choose from numerous dining options that adjoin the casino, go shopping, enjoy lounge entertainment or shows, or continue the journey in the tropics by visiting the property's "dolphinarium" or the white tigers. Indeed, the integration of live animals to (dis)simulate the experience of nature has become increasingly common in resort-casino design.

10. The Grand Canal at The Venetian. Immersive spectacles entice onlookers and participants into performing the
property's theme, in this instance for $16 a rider.

(Mis)reading Cityscapes

Just across the Strip from The Mirage, the dissimulated rupture between the real and its representation is elevated
to a *raison d'etre* at Paris and The Venetian. Paris and Venice are among the most romantic cities in popular
American imagination, hosting multiple layers of history, culture, and slick sophistication. Their *genius loci* have made
them attractive settings for novels and movies, bequeathing strong popular images of what these cities must be like.
Both have distinguishing landmarks that are recognized instantly all over the world. Popular imagination renders their
alleyways and plazas exciting, full of shops, cafés, restaurants, and opportunities for cultural exploration. In Pseurope,
the reproduction of these cityscapes ties the non-gaming amenities directly to the overall theme.

Paris and The Venetian cater to these expectations of shopping, dining, and street life—staples of the European
middle-class everyday—at a convenient scale. As the visitor moves indoors through the monumental façades, the
journey becomes more intimate. The alleys of the two properties have small shops and boutiques, bars and restaurants, barber shops, lampposts, bridges, and benches. They are carefully configured for people-watching (and for
people-displaying), as there is plenty of space to sit, the dining areas open to the "street," and crowds mill around,
just as in real cities. The space is busy but lacks a sense of congestion. Sophisticated lighting systems employing
careful placement and direction, color filters, and other special visual effects support the atmosphere. Music and
other acoustical phenomena enhance the patrons' "travel experience."[66] In Paris, it is the happy accordion sound of
the 1920s, the theme's time frame. In The Venetian, it is classical music and opera and an occasional performance
by a singing gondolier. Indeed, gondola rides are available on the Grand Canal—which runs through the property,
just by St. Mark's Square—for $16, although compared with Venice, Italy, it is a bargain (figure 10).

The scene and the details at Paris and The Venetian keep the visitor curious for hours. Both properties claim to be
realistic replicas of real cities, so they invite comparisons, regardless of whether the visitor has been in Europe. Not
surprisingly, these resort-casinos "prove only as accurate as the stereotypes [they are] built upon and the messy
realities [they] exclude."[67] The resultant fact that many things about these places are "not quite right" is not necessarily
disturbing, but sometimes just an amusing part of the entertainment experience. At best, they are both. Or what should
one think about a sign on the wall in Paris, Las Vegas, saying, "The cobblestone street you are about to enter is a
re-creation of an authentic Paris street. It is an uneven surface. Therefore please watch your step."?

Either way, the divergences between the real cities and their frequently surreal Las Vegas replicas (e.g., the Venice
in Las Vegas has *two* St. Mark's Squares) can be so extreme as to shatter the suspension of disbelief entirely and

11. The sky of the Forum Shops at Caesars Palace. The resort-casino lays claim over time as well as place, turning day to night and back again every hour on the hour.

compel subversive reading. For example, despite its many charms, the real Venice can be smelly and verminous. The piazzas are crowded with pigeons. Rats ford the canals, and the narrow medieval alleys can be redolent of the urban effluence and rotting algae that intermittently choke the surrounding lagoon. For its part, the streets of Paris, France, are filled with people from all walks of life, not only the tidy, wealthy citizen-consumers. The contemporary Las Vegas patrons, however, do not evince overmuch discontent with the exclusion of these elements from their recreational spaces. Other disappearances, however, can become a serious matter from the customer's perspective. The absence of bookstores, for instance. In the words of a disappointed European visitor to Paris, Las Vegas, "And what kind of Paris doesn't have bookstores??! In the *real* Paris, they would be everywhere!" Even in a city where the word *book* usually has nothing to do with reading, this *is* disturbing.

Such selectively edited stereotypes and strategically deployed absences point to troublesome issues outside the resort-casino's narrative. In the Venice of the Adriatic, for instance, one fascinating narrative legible to an observant visitor is how mountains of tourist-generated garbage are transported through the narrow alleys and out along the canals. But at The Venetian, mountains of left-over restaurant food simply vanish into dumpsters concealed somewhere behind the anonymous back exits. Similarly, there are no *miserables* nor bureaucratic brusqueness at Paris, Las Vegas, just as there were no references to political instability or postcolonial restiveness at the Aladdin casino-resort—the increasingly uncomfortable and often remarked-upon lacunae come after the violent geopolitical eruptions of late 2001 onward.[68] These narrative lacunae are vital and, indeed, a prerequisite to securing a univocally interpreted resort-casino narrative of optimal salability.[69] But such sanitized narratives are also jarring and potentially self-subverting by reason of their referring to real social and political milieus that may diverge radically and unromantically from their Vegas counterparts.

Similarly revealing and potentially as jarring are the questions of who is fair game to be themed and then sold to whom. The era of "fauxriental" themes appears to be subsiding. The folkways of such places as China are no longer objects of amusement but something to be taken seriously, lest one run the risk of alienating some of the Strip's high-stakes gamblers. Properties hosting many Chinese customers have removed the unlucky number four from the hotel floor count and elevator panels. The era of drinks served up in "Buddha" mugs with rubbable bellies is over.

But some sensitivities are less equal than others. At The Voodoo Lounge atop the Rio, walls are decorated with *vèvè*—sacred Vodoun cosmograms—scattered about in contexts and adjacencies that practitioners of this living religion would consider grossly inappropriate.[70] Likewise, the cocktail selection is a compendium of Hollywood's most derogatory anti-Vodoun stereotypes, packed with references to zombification and shrunken heads. The Voodoo Lounge, then, is akin to a Catholic-themed watering hole with crucifixes imprinted on the carpet, or a *faux* kosher pub called, perhaps, the Bar Mitzvah where Bloody Marys are wittily renamed for the blood libel. In the displaced places of the resort-casino, then, one is entitled to only as much derision-free self-representation as one can afford. For the foreseeable future, the European package tourist and East Asian high roller trump the Caribbean agriculturist.

Displacement in the resort-casino, however, is not exclusively a matter of the representational distortion of temporally and spatially distant locales; rather, it is equally a matter of what is immediately outside the casino's walls. Integral to many of these properties' atmosphere of displacement is their artificial sky, a feature that has become a staple in the themed resort-casino (figure 11). This sky represents "a hybrid cultural artifact that combines business enterprise, amusement park, tourist attraction, engineering feat, and technological experiment to produce a controlled environment within a monumental urban space."[71] It manipulates time and space in a sophisticated manner, bringing in the outside and overcoming the 24-hour day by cycling from day to night at hourly intervals. It "controls perspective and perception by making the clouds appear as if they were moving when one walks [the 'street'] underneath. This artifact 'seems to suggest that the outside world has been obviated, transcended, or replaced.'"[72] Yet what is under control is "*human* nature," rather than nature: the artificial sky attracts people into the property, holds their interest, and offers "a refuge, an attractive alternative to the threatening and chaotic world outside."[73, 74] The sky supports the fantasy of a journey and even stimulates the desire for it. The sky thus points to the resort-casino designs' understanding of simulacra. Authenticity is irrelevant, "but signification is the most important in examining the spatial and ideological narrative articulated in the interiorized, urban wilderness" of the desert city's cities and jungles.[75]

The artificial sky exemplifies the fusion of gaming and entertainment within a logic of total simulation.[76] This fusion makes it easier to include more amenities and enhance the property's identity through dining and shopping. Reflective of the change is that many celebrity chefs now work in Las Vegas and are components of its live entertainments. These multiple layers of the Strip's entertainmentscape accommodate a variety of desires. In the words of a casino president, Las Vegas is "an entertainment capital now, not just a gambling capital."[77]

But When the Chips Are Down…
Las Vegas is still a gambling town. The Strip casinos have thousands of slot machines and gaming tables that accept a great variety of stakes. The popularity of slot machines increased dramatically with the proliferation of the gaming

12. The gaming-area carpet at New York–New York relates simultaneously to property themes and player comfort in fine detail.

industry as new gamblers entered the market and the design of the devices evolved.[78] Many of these new customers were perhaps relatively inexperienced, but learned to demand and discriminate as they were exposed to interactive video games and televised and online poker tournaments and could choose from several gambling destinations. To attract this market, Las Vegas extended its design principles to the casino floor. The goal there, too, was to make a strong brand statement and attract and entertain the customers—and keep them playing as long as possible.

Sophisticated signage is one way to bring the customer into the gaming area. The interactive, three-dimensional signs above themed groups of slot machines are programmed to respond to slot activity. When somebody wins, the signs add to the excitement with flashing lights, elaborate graphics, movement, and perky sound effects. Together with the jubilant cheers of the winner, the signage catches people's attention. The area fills up quickly, and a few observers decide to stay nearby, for these machines must be *lucky*. Indeed, it has been shown that gamblers are very superstitious.[79]

Only physically comfortable gamblers will keep playing. The carpet under their feet must be durable to meet the demands of a 24-7 business and Nevada's strict fire safety laws, but soft enough to maximize comfort. Its colors and patterns need to provide a momentary refuge, but not distract the eyes away from the game for too long (figure 12). Chairs are particularly important, because numb legs will make people leave. Sometimes, pleasant scents are added to the air. Investigations into a scent's impact on consumer behavior confirm that particular odors stimulate people to gamble or shop.[80] On top of all this, the gamblers' drinks are free, but their delivery may take a while.

The greater diversity of customers and the increased popularity of slot machines put pressure on the table games, which many inexperienced players found confusing and even intimidating. This circumstance led to a search for simpler and more exciting table games and, most importantly, for ways of "setting the mood for table play."[81] The once stoic dealers are now encouraged to interact with the customer. A relaxed atmosphere and good service lengthen the time the customers spend at the tables and are more likely to bring them back. Dealers still need precise technical skills, but they are also expected to entertain, teach, and do their share of the marketing by adding a human touch. Their "job description nowadays is to be outgoing, outgoing, outgoing."[82]

The space itself is equally important as the activity. Many casinos have installed "mini-roofs" above the tables "to break up the space."[83] They provide a sense of sheltering enclosure and, not incidentally, an armature for observation cameras (figure 6). Carpeting, lighting, and theming support the sense of intimacy. The theme is confirmed further through custom-made cards, dice, tables, and tokens (chips) that promote special occasions and tempt as souvenirs. In general, the details, comfort, and convenience of the setting reflect the level of stakes wagered: "the higher the limits, the cushier the seat."[84]

The intimacy of table games is important in their appeal to certain customer segments. The wealthy Generation Xers, many of whom grew up playing video games and now hold white-collar jobs, find table games particularly appealing. Internationally televised poker tournaments and online gambling have added to their popularity. Some want a break from life at the computer, because "they get so much of using computers and the Internet as a part of their everyday life that they don't consider it a part of human recreation."[85] For many of these players, live gambling is simply a "cool" alternative to online activities as well as something to be enjoyed with a fine drink and a cigar (available at the cigar shop adjacent to the gambling area). Evoking Hollywood representations of the Rat Pack's Las Vegas, table games underscore style, image, and even self-aggrandizement and intensify the sensual and social experience.[86] At the tables, the narrative of the space thus lets the gambler be the maverick, high-rolling hero of the story.

Conclusion: A Geography of Paradox
The imagineered worlds on the Las Vegas Strip are a response to the city's inner dynamics and global and nation-wide social and economic forces, most notably the proliferation of gambling. Embeddedness in changing social processes at multiple spatial scales strongly informs the contemporary Strip, but the Strip has turned these forces back upon themselves through a wizardly manipulation of scale, along with other basic concepts of geography. To compete successfully in a cutthroat market, Las Vegas has compressed the world by replicating some of its best (or most saleable) offerings in one place. In doing so, it has injected a feverish sense of journey (movement) in the entertainment experience. The credibility of this ersatz excursion within a few city blocks depends on the artful imagineering of space and time—on the successful twisting of the visitors' perceptual boundaries. The landscape thus becomes one of continuous displacement, a dense zone of fluctuating, simulated space-time transitions. This concept is the case at every scale, regardless of whether one stands on the Strip, inside the resort-casino, or between rows of slot machines.

This displacement effect has a larger agenda as well. It is carefully produced and strategically deployed to sever visitors from the mundane and re-place them within prefabricated narratives of the fantastic. The white tigers, artificial skies, quaint streetscapes, and lush tropical gardens exemplify how this techne of displacement relies upon the confusion of the outside and the inside, the excluded, and its filtered re-inclusion. Even the location of Las Vegas is made complicit in this experience of displacement: the contrast between the desert and the Strip's tweaked landscapes of abundance creates a sense of distance that supports the successful suspension of disbelief. It is no surprise, then, that Las Vegas once marketed itself with the slogan "Freedom From Reality,"[87] phrased as though it were a constitutional right.

But displacement from the real and re-placement within the fantastic necessarily entails displacing the not-so-fantastic to the outside. Thus, freedom from reality for some necessitates banishment to reality for others and perhaps an enslavement of the real itself. Simulation dissimulates, and in the Strip's simulated worlds, it is their unpleasant underpinning reality that is dissimulated through displacement. Thus, the resort-casino carefully conceals its heavy reliance upon environmental depredation, its hunger for exploitable labor, and its overarching imperative to expropriate visitors' cash. The Strip's mechanisms for creating a very postmodern, heterogeneous recreational experience are therefore very modern and industrially homogeneous. There is a powerful illusion of freedom, and the city's marketing suggests that "anything goes" (while, of course, staying in Vegas), but a strict separation is maintained between the imagineered, its requisite infrastructure, and its excluded others. In the resort-casino, for example, customers are carefully separated from the casinos' operational spaces (surveillance, maintenance, count rooms, and so on) and from other customer segments according to their respective credit lines. The eye is constantly redirected toward the stories the casinos want the customers to read and purchase, but rewriting is discouraged. A tight rein (of seduction, distraction, and, if necessary, coercion) is kept on those who might perform the stories divergently and, in so doing, harm profitability. The packaging and sale of variety, then, necessarily entails the preclusion of difference.[88] Therefore, the endless difference and uniqueness in which the customers are supposed to indulge are neither different nor particularly unique upon closer inspection. Rather, they are the highly standardized output of thematically differentiated leisure factories in which difference in any meaningful sense is barred so as to ensure that nothing is accidental. In this hedonistic reality-free utopia, manipulation and exclusion strive for instrumental control over the individual's behavior and relationship with the environment.

In our opinion, it is this particular geography of paradox that explains why time out on the Strip so excites and bores. Too much manufactured and antiseptic variety becomes monotonous. It is all different, and it is all the same.[89] After the initial excitement wears thin, this monotonous excess undermines the willing suspension of disbelief by becoming transparent—promoting "misreadings" and inciting the irruption of counternarratives. Perhaps the most fascinating twist to this geography, then, is the democracy of its authoritarianism—and the authoritarianism of its democracy.

The beauty and bestiality are in the beholder's eye; the better these work together, the more seamless the resort-casino experience feels and the more oppressively manufactured and regulated it is. This contradiction guarantees that counternarratives remain possible, probable, and even legibly pre-inscribed in even the most perfectly themed settings. The multiplicity of authorized (and especially unauthorized) stories also explains what draws us to willingly and frequently gorge upon the Strip: we get sick of it, stampede back home, and then cannot resist the need to go back.

Notes

This article builds upon Steven Flusty and Pauliina Raento 's 2006 "Three Trips to Italy: Deconstructing the New Las Vegas," in *Travels in Paradox: Remapping Tourism*, eds. C. Minca and T. Oakes (Lanham: Rowman and Littlefield, 2006), 97–124. Dr. Raento's contribution is related to her Academy of Finland-funded research project "Landscapes, Icons, and Images" (2008–12).

1 Carpenter, E. *On What a Blow That Phantom Gave Me!* (New York: Holt, Rinehart, and Winstop, 1974), 180.

2 Klein, N. M. "The Politics of Scripted Places: Las Vegas and Reno." *Nevada Historical Society Quarterly* (40), 1997, 151–159; Kranes, D. "Play Grounds." *Journal of Gambling Studies* (11), 1995, 91–102; "Story Spaces: Any Casino's Romance and How It's Told." *The Business of Gaming*, eds. Eadington, W. R. and Cornelius, J. A. (Reno: University of Nevada Institute for the Study of Gambling and Commercial Gaming, 1999), 291–302; and "The Primal Player and the New-Millennium Casino." Paper presented at the 11th International Conference on Gambling and Risk-Taking (Las Vegas, Nevada), June 13–16, 2000.

3 Kranes. 1999, 294.

4 Klein. 1997, 151. Klein, N. M. *The Vatican to Vegas: A History of Special Effects* (New York: The New Press, 2004), 338.

5 Christiansen, E. and Brinkerhoff-Jacobs, J. "The Relationship of Gaming to Entertainment." *Gambling*, eds. Eadington, W. A. and Cornelius, J. A. (Reno: University of Nevada Institute for the Study of Gambling and Commercial Gaming, 1997), 11–48.

6 Raento, P. and Douglass, W. A. "The Naming of Gaming." *Names* (49), 2001, 1–35.

7 Barthes, R. "The Death of the Author." *Image, Music, Text* (New York: Hill and Wang, 1977).

8 *Encore Las Vegas.* Completed in 2008 for $2.3 billion. For more price tags, see the Hotel/Casino Development Construction Bulletin at *www.lvcva.com*. Last accessed on June 6, 2010.

9 For these stories, consult *The Real Las Vegas: Life beyond the Strip*, ed. Littlejohn, D. (Oxford and New York: Oxford University Press, 1999); *The Grit beneath the Glitter: Tales from the Real Las Vegas*, eds.

Rothman, H. K. and Davis, M. (Berkeley: University of California Press, 2002); Mullen, J. M. *Las Vegas: Media and Myth* (Plymouth: Lexington Books, 2007).

10 Slogan cited in Voigt, J. "R&R Lets Freedom Ring in Vegas: $40 Mil. Branding Campaign Stays Away from Slots and Showgirls." *AdWeek*, September 25, 2000, 6.

11 Moehring, E. P. *Resort City in the Sunbelt*, 2nd ed. (Reno: University of Nevada Press, 2000), 49.

12 See Wolfe, T. *The Kandy-Kolored Tangerine-Flaked Streamlined Baby* (New York: Farrar, Straus & Giroux, 1965), 10–11; Findlay, J. M. *People of Chance* (New York: Oxford University Press, 1986), 136–152; Smith, J. F. "Bugsy's Flamingo and the Modern Casino-Hotel." *Gambling and Public Policy*, eds. Eadington, W. R. and Cornelius, J. A. (Reno: University of Nevada Institute for the Study of Gambling and Commercial Gaming, 1991), 499–518; Schwartz, D. G. *Suburban Xanadu* (New York and

London: Routledge, 2003).

13 Moehring. 2000, 117.

14 See also Raento and Douglass. 2001, 15.

15 Moehring. 2000, 116–118.

16 See *Variations on a Theme Park: The New American City and the End of Public Space*, ed. Sorkin, M. (New York: The Noonday Press, 1992); Gottdiener, M. *The Theming of America: American Dreams, Media Fantasies, and Themed Environments* (Boulder: Westview, 1997); Clavé, S. A. *The Global Theme Park Industry* (Oxfordshire and Cambridge: CABI, 2007).

17 Smith. 1991, 508–509.

18 Spanier, D. Welcome to the Pleasuredome (Reno: University of Nevada Press, 1992), 35.

19 Spanier. 1992, 33.

20 Cited in Spanier. 1992, 33.

21 Historical Las Vegas Visitor Statistics at *www.lvcva.com*. Last accessed on June 6, 2010.

22 The Historical Las Vegas Visitor Statistics records 4.5 million delegates attending a convention in Las Vegas in 2009. The peak year was 2006, with 6.3 million conventioneers. The one-million mark was crossed in 1984.

23 Annual visitation statistics from the Historical Las Vegas Visitor Statistics; visitor demographics from *Las Vegas Visitor Profile Study*. Las Vegas Visitor and Convention Authority. 2009, 81–82; 1999, 82–83; 1991, 59–60.

24 *Las Vegas Visitor Profile Study*. 2009, 43, 77; 1999, 40, 79; 1991, 26, 56.

25 Historical Las Vegas Visitor Statistics. Answers to frequently asked questions about Las Vegas may be found at *www.lvcva.com*. Last accessed on June 6, 2010.

26 *Las Vegas Visitor Profile Study*. 2009, 61, 66; 1999, 59, 70; 1991, 42, 50.

27 *Las Vegas Visitor Profile Study*. 2009, 58, 60; 1999, 55, 57; 1991, 39, 41.

28 Casino president cited in Palermo, D. "The Great White Way Heads West." *International Gaming & Wagering Business 20 (7)*. 1999, 43.

29 *Las Vegas Visitor Profile Study*. 2009, 82; 1999, 83; 1991, 60.

30 See *www.nynyhotelcasino.com*. Last accessed on June 6, 2010.

31 Kranes. 1999, 297.

32 Kranes. 1999, 292; see also Gottdiener, M. and Lagopoulos, A. *The City and the Sign* (New York: Columbia University Press, 1986).

33 Legato, F. "Signs of the Times." *Casino Journal 11 (*3*).* 1998, 82.

34 Klein. 2004.

35 Cited in Klepacki, L. "Signs of the Times." *International Gaming & Wagering Business* 18 (1). 1997, 48.

36 Venturi, R., Brown, D. S. and Izenour, S. *Learning from Las Vegas* (Cambridge: MIT Press, 1972). Also see *Relearning from Las Vegas*, eds. Vinegar, A. and Golec. M. J. (Minneapolis: University of Minnesota Press, 2009).

37 Sign designer cited in Klepacki. 1997, 50.

38 See Raento and Douglass. 2001, 8–9.

39 See *www.citycenter.com*. For promotional videos, consult *http://citycenter.thedigitalcenter. com/projects/1293-citycentermedia-gallery*. Last accessed on June 6, 2010.

40 Raento and Douglass. 2001, 8. See also Eco, U. *Travels in Hyper-reality* (San Diego: Harcourt Brace Jovanovich, 1986).

41 We coined the term *Pseurope* in Raento and Flusty. 2006, 117.

42 See Crawford, M. "The World in a Shopping Mall." *Variations on a Theme Park: The New American City and the End of Public Space,* ed. Sorkin, M. (New York: The Noonday Press, 1992), 3–30.

43 Venturi et al. 1972.

44 Tuan, Y-F. "Space and Place: Humanistic Perspective." *Progress in Geography (*6*).* 1975, 236.

45 Crawford. 1992, 14.

46 Flusty, S. *DeCocaColonization: Making the Globe from the Inside Out.* (London and New York: Routledge, 2004), see chapter four; Sorkin. 1992.

47 Sign designer cited in Klepacki. 1997, 50.

48 Kranes. 1999.

49 Casino manager cited in "Projects of Distinction." *International Gaming & Wagering Business* (18). 1997, 42.

50 Klein. 2004, 331.

51 Classen, C., Howes, D. and Synnott, A. *Aroma* (London: Routledge, 1994), 192–197, 203–205; Hirsch, A. R. "Effects of Ambient Odors on Slot-Machine Usage in a Las Vegas Casino." *Psychology & Marketing* (12). 1995, 585–594; Smith, G. W. "Tuft Decisions." *International Gaming & Wagering Business* 18 (9). 1997, 78–79.

52 Kranes. 1995, 94–95.

53 Casino architect cited in International Gaming & Wagering Business (IGWB). 1997, 45.

54 Kranes. 1995 and 2000.

55 IGWB. 1997, 45.

56 Casino architect cited in Parets, R. T. "Making a Grand Entrance." *IGWB* 19 (11). 1998, 20.

57 Parets. 1998, 24.

58 Parets. 1998, 22; see also Kranes. 1995, 94.

59 See *www.mirage.com/attractions/aquarium.aspx*. Last accessed on June 6, 2010.

60 See Raento and Douglass. 2001, 15–16. For a full list, see *www.mirage.com/meetings/meeting-rooms.aspx*. Last accessed on June 6, 2010.

61 Hausladen, G. *Places for Dead Bodies*. (Austin: University of Texas Press, 2000), 27.

62 Preservation specialist cited in Quinn, W. "The Finishing Touch." *Casino Journal* 11 (8). 1998, 70.

63 Preservation specialist cited in Quinn. 1998, 73.

64 Spanier. 1992, 35.

65 Kranes. 1995, 99.

66 Grant, A. "Making the Property Worth Seeing." *Casino Journal* 12 (6). 1999, 84.

67 Raento and Flusty. 2006, 117.

68 On Las Vegas in the context of resurgent militarism, see Flusty, S. "Empire of the Insensate." *Indefensible Space: The Architecture of the National Insecurity State,* ed. Sorkin, M. (New York and London: Routledge, 2008), 29–50.

69 Raento and Douglass. 2001, 10.

70 See *www.destination360. com/north-america/us/nevada/ las-vegas/rio-voodoo-lounge#*. Last accessed on May 24, 2010.

71 Branch, M. P. "Cosmology in the Casino: Simulacra of Nature in the Interiorized Wilderness." *The Nature of Cities,* eds. Bennett, M. and Teague, D. W. (Tucson: The University of Arizona Press, 1999), 277–298.

72 Branch. 1999, 287. Cited by Raento and Flusty. 2006, 107.

73 Branch. 1999, 291 (emphasis in original). Cited by Raento and Flusty 2006, 108.

74 Branch. 1999, 292. See also Kranes. 1995, 94–95; Klein. 1997, 154, 157.

75 Branch. 1999, 289. See also Raento and Flusty. 2006, 110. For an argument about Las Vegas being "its own authentic reality," see Douglass, W. A. and Raento, P. "The Tradition of Invention: Conceiving Las Vegas." *Annals of Tourism Research* (31). 2004, 7–23.

76 Christiansen and Brinkerhoff-Jacobs. 1997.

77 Cited in Palermo. 1999, 43.

78 Findlay. 1986, 207; Spanier. 1992, 187–193; Dickerson, M. "Why 'Slots' Equals 'Grind' in Any Language: The Cross-Cultural Popularity of the Slot Machine." *Gambling Cultures,* ed. McMillen, J. (London: Routledge, 1996), 152–166. *Las Vegas Visitor Profile Study.* 2009, 63; 1991, 45. Seventy percent of visitors to Las Vegas favored slots in 2009 compared to 49% in 1991.

79 See Walker, M. B. "Irrational Thinking among Slot Machine Players." *Journal of Gambling Studies* (8). 1992, 245–261; Spanier, D. *Inside the Gambler's Mind* (Reno: University of Nevada Press, 1994), 152–168; Griffiths, M. and Bingham, C. "A Psychological Study of Bingo Players and Their Superstitious Beliefs." Paper presented at the 11th International Conference on Gambling and Risk-Taking (Las Vegas, Nevada), June 13–16, 2000.

80 Classen et al. 1994, 192–197; Hirsch. 1995.

81 Weinert, J. "Setting the table" *IGWB* 18 (8). 1997, 45.

82 Dealer educator cited in Hogan, B. A. "The Personal Touch." *IGWB* 18 (8). 1997, 42.

83 Casino designer cited in Weinert. 1997, 45.

84 Weinert. 1997, 45.

85 Casino executive cited in Berns, D. "Back to the Future." *IGWB* 19 (10). 1998, 20.

86 See Goffman, E. "Where the Action Is." *Interaction Ritual* (New York: Pantheon, 1967), 149–270; Marksbury, R. A. "Ethnography in a Casino: Social Dynamics at Blackjack Tables." *Global Gambling: Cultural Perspectives on Gambling Organizations,* ed. Kingma, S. F. (London and New York: Routledge, 2010), 91–112.

87 This was in 2002.

88 Flusty, S. "The Banality of Interdiction: Surveillance, Control, and the Displacement of Diversity." *International Journal of Urban and Regional Research* (25). 2001, 658-664. See also Cook, I. and Crang, P. "The World on a Plate: Culinary Culture, Displacement, and Geographical Knowledges." *Journal of Material Culture* (1). 1996, 131–153, especially 145.

89 See also Spanier. 1992, 1. Cited in Raento and Flusty. 2006, 97.

LAS VEGAS
TODAY

Las Vegas officials Excerpts from discussions with Alan M. Feldman, senior vice president of public affairs, MGM Mirage, and Brian Yost, vice president of resort development, Harrah's Entertainment, with comments from Oscar Goodman, mayor of Las Vegas.

Alan M. Feldman Las Vegas must be placed in context. Otherwise, people may easily believe someone stood at one end of the Strip and said, "Let's build one casino that looks like a castle, one that looks like Italy, and one that looks like a little metropolis," as if it were all planned in one shot—just add water, shake, and *boom*. Of course that is not at all how Las Vegas developed.

In 1905, Las Vegas was thriving as a train stop but not yet as a city. Its development formally began on May 15, 1905, when 1,200 lots of land were auctioned at Boulder Junction—the blocks immediately adjacent to Fremont Street in what is known today as downtown Las Vegas. To the south, the city's boundaries extended to Sahara Boulevard, beyond which and all along the famous Strip the land is part of Clark County.

With deregulation in 1931, a business could obtain an unlimited gaming license, that allowed for the installation of slot machines and table games in conjunction with building hotels with at least three hundred rooms. The original Strip hotels date from the 1940s and include the Sands, the Dunes, the Flamingo, and the Sahara, which all started as 300-room hotels. In some cases, the buildings were motels with exterior corridors and bare-bone fixtures; a box up front would comprise slot machines, a coffee shop, and often a simple theater but little infrastructure.

Howard Hughes and Bugsy Siegel often are mentioned as founding fathers of Las Vegas, but I'm not convinced Siegel is worthy of the label. What Siegel envisioned on the Strip was the development of a larger casino, an idea that was not possible within the boundaries of downtown Las Vegas. But his casino was an absolute mess when it first opened. To me, the founding fathers of Las Vegas are really Jay Sarno, Kurt Korkorian, and Steve Wynn. Sarno had a gut instinct, an intuition about the way Las Vegas worked that no one before and few after him had. Sadly, his personal issues—a gambling addict, alcoholic, and inveterate womanizer—hampered his success. Even though some of the properties he created still stand, when Sarno owned them, they were unable to realize their potential. He left Las Vegas in 1974, promising to return to build the largest, most ambitious hotel of them all: the Grandissimo. In the end, he could find no willing partners.

However, in the early 1960s, Sarno created a resort in which customers were in complete control, kings of their own world engrossed in an unrivaled fantasy experience. He chose Rome for his fantasy theme: his guests would be caesars, and Caesars Palace became one of the first themed hotels in Las Vegas, opening in August 1966. He started a trend on the Strip of setting everything back from the street rather than developing right to the curb. By comparison, right across from Caesars, the Flamingo Hotel allows about fourteen feet between the curb and its first slot machine.

Out front, Sarno placed a fountain and planted the now towering cypress trees, creating a wonderful entrance experience, a sequential moment, that evolved from the outside to the extravagant interior. Inside and to the left was Circus Maximus and the showroom, straight ahead was the casino, and to the right was a space for the future creation of a slot room called Circus Circus. There, he planned to install the not-yet-popular slot machines, but he never got that far—he had to sell Caesars Palace. With the funds received from the Caesars transaction, he developed a new fantasy themed resort: Circus Circus. Guests would play under a big-top tent with circus acts. In front of the property, he articulated an arrival experience. While acrobats in flight overhead was an exciting spectacle, gamblers at the tables were freaked out. Like Caesars before it, Circus Circus faltered financially. Sarno ended up selling it to his accountants, Bill Pennington and Bill Bennett, who turned the property around and used it as the basis to develop Circus Circus Enterprises, which eventually developed Excalibur, Luxor, and Mandalay Bay. In 2004, MGM purchased Mandalay Resort Group, which is now part of MGM Resorts International. As the man who brought the concept of fantasy to life in Las Vegas, Jay Sarno is worthy of the "founding father" description.

Kirk Kerkorian is another self-made entrepreneur in Las Vegas. After success in the airline, freight, and movie businesses, he began investing in the hotel-and-casino industry in the 1940s. Kerkorian envisioned hotels far larger and more complex than had his predecessors; he single-handedly developed the concept of the Las Vegas scale.

While the original hotels on the Strip each had three hundred rooms, a small number were beginning to get somewhat larger; Caesars and the Sands had about six hundred rooms. In the mid 1960s, Kerkorian began to develop the 1,000-room Las Vegas International, later to become the Las Vegas Hilton. At the time, no 1,000-room hotels existed in America or in the world, but Kerkorian saw that Las Vegas could exist at a scale not possible in the rest of country. In 1973, he built the largest hotel in Las Vegas at the time, the 2,000-room MGM Grand, which today is Ballys Hotel. In 1994, not willing to be outdone, as 3,000-room hotels were becoming commonplace (including the expanded Las Vegas Hilton), he built a 5,000-room hotel, the MGM Grand. Having proven Las Vegas could sustain hotels of size and complexity unknown in any other part of the world, Kirk Kerkorian deserves to be called a

CityCenter under construction, Las Vegas

I would never have had the courage to build these casinos as they have been built. Now they cost over a billion dollars! Further, as soon as you dig a spade into the ground, you know that, just a little way down the Strip, someone is building a resort bigger or better than yours.
— Oscar Goodman, mayor of Las Vegas

Las Vegas founding father. While the city's development absorbed these economies of fantasy and scale, next came Steve Wynn's concept of quality.

Many people believe Wynn's 1989 Mirage introduced a new paradigm into Las Vegas's culture. I was with the team that opened The Mirage, and I am not sure we had such lofty notions, but we believed we were continuing Sarno's concept of creating a fantasy experience. The Sarno influence is easily seen in the hotel's tropical-themed entrance experience replete with a rainforest and palm trees.

There are similarities between the plan of the original Ceasars Palace and that of The Mirage, especially in the relationship between the casino and the non-gaming amenities. The casino served as a central gathering point, as a kind of a plaza, surrounded by restaurants and the showroom itself. The fundamental relationships among the spaces were first established by Jay Sarno in 1966; Steve Wynn gave them new life and considerably larger levels of investment in 1989. Caesars Palace was developed with millions of dollars, the infamous Teamsters' pension money; in contrast, by 1989, The Mirage investment reached $611 million.

After Wynn's company, Mirage Resorts, developed The Mirage, Treasure Island, and then the Bellagio, the concept of quality and sophistication solidified. The Bellagio became the first Las Vegas hotel to receive an AAA five-diamond rating (the highest hotel rating in its system). The luxury included specially designed fountains that spurted water to music. As the six-billion-dollar pinnacle of resorts at the time, the hotel added more convention space and more rooms. However, the hotel-casino paradigm had not yet completely changed.

Today, business in Las Vegas is not limited to the casino. In 1968, the casino clearly generated the lion's share of a property's revenue. The motto was, even if stuff has to be given away, "fill the rooms, and they will fill the slot machines." Gradually, the revenue model changed, and by 1984, the city enhanced Sunday-to-Thursday business by offering amenities such as convention centers, wedding chapels, and retail. Further, while revenue from entertainment shows and retail was minimal in the 1970s, between 1989, when The Mirage opened, and 2007, the average room rate had quadrupled, not because of inflation but because the rooms were of excellent quality, and people spend money on better quality.

However, as the city has become less dependent on gaming, the revenue from gambling itself has not decreased. In fact, the total pie is growing more rapidly in other areas: In 1970, $1.1 billion of the city's total revenue came from gaming, but in 2007 it rose to almost $2 billion.

In 2004, our company questioned how to make productive the acreage between the Bellagio and the Monte Carlo. We were not going to install an eight-acre lake, but we did develop a six-acre retail area that is intended to be both profitable and animate the spaces. CityCenter is not what Bugsy Siegel nor Howard Hughes imagined; rather, it is a place that has evolved through the leadership of MGM Chairman Jim Murren as well as the combined visions of many architects and designers who contributed to make this project what it is today: the most ambitious resort on the Strip and the largest privately funded construction project in the United States today.

A 1955 *Life* magazine article noted, "Set for its biggest boom, Vegas is pushing its luck." The article claimed the boom had reached its height; however, this claim has been made and remade every decade since. However, the entrepreneurial energy of Las Vegas keeps coming up with ways of reinventing the city. In 2004, as we approached the design of CityCenter, we realized it had to be a reflection of a new Las Vegas, one in which the old paradigm of reliance on casino revenue could be reinvented.

This 18 million-square-foot urban destination resort was well under way when the Great Recession of 2008 took hold. By 2009, the flailing national economy had an enormous impact on the performance of Las Vegas properties, with spending down on food, gaming, entertainment, and retail. Despite this, the city's overall visitation only dropped by three percentage points, and, in December 2009, MGM Mirage successfully opened CityCenter. Because we were trying to respond to new opportunities in the market, CityCenter included a residential component. While this was a first for a Las Vegas Strip property, once the details of CityCenter were announced in 2004, several similar projects followed.

Now, in early 2010, even though the market for real estate has been dreadful, we are certain there will be demand and the Strip will continue to evolve. As a result, while sales aren't tracking anywhere near the expectations of 2004, buyers are closing on their units and new purchasers regularly present themselves.

The Great Recession has had severe impacts on some of these projects: Echelon by Boyd Gaming has been put on indefinite hold. The Fountainbleau project has been stopped completely, sold in bankruptcy The Cosmopolitan, which started development as a condo and casino/hotel, has eliminated the condos and is struggling to open the casino/hotel.

While new development may not be seen for several years, Las Vegas is still evolving. Casino operators will continue to look for ways to keep their properties energized and invigorated. New restaurants, shows, nightclubs, retailers,

For us to be a world-class city we need a
world-class major league sports franchise.
— Oscar Goodman

and room designs will drive this process for the next decade. Major investment in new developments will return after the financial markets heal. Despite oft-repeated predictions to the contrary, Las Vegas is nowhere close to being finished.

Brian Yost A benchmark year for Harrah's in Las Vegas was 2004, the first year non-gaming revenue surpassed gaming revenue. In fact, this was true for the overall Las Vegas market.

Generation X and Generation Y consumers are important to us not only because they will become a greater percentage of overall spenders, but because their spending power is much more heavily weighted in non-gaming than gaming spending. This characteristic of Gen X and Gen Y spending patterns is more influential to where we focus content and programming than what makes these consumers important. The fact that they are a growing and an underserved market makes them attractive.

Suddenly, the visitor experience is paramount and will drive the bottom line. If the experience is well-orchestrated, guests will be compelled to participate and profits will flow.

What should be developed today within Caesars when there are already three Cartier stores? How many more Cartier stores can Las Vegas handle? Not a lot. For an industry that averages $500 to $600 per square foot, the Forum Shops at Caesars Palace are the highest-grossing retail square footage in the world at just under $1,500 per square foot. How can the programming be different? In considering a new development to the east of Las Vegas Boulevard, we have to make common spaces that are completely different than anything that exists in the market today.

We are interested in social networking in the sense of providing opportunities for the people who come to Las Vegas in groups of two or more to stay connected with each other and the products Harrah's offers, as well as make new friends and hang out with like-minded people.

Las Vegas was built on the wallets of the baby boomers, who still retain a level of disposable income to make the city a viable economic model for years to come; therefore, new developments must be pleasing to them as well. I am not at all advocating program homogenization but rather a program mix accessible to consumers outside of our target audience, so they don't go to our competitors. Basically, this strategy is an exercise in filtering against the target audience without going so far as to alienate the larger consumer market.

Today, Las Vegas is not a comfortable environment for pedestrians, so we are putting an emphasis on a place that is comfortable. We envision a "greenscape" and pleasant spaces for people to walk through. Further, we are focused on improving the visitor experience by alleviating the conflict between the automobile and the pedestrian.

Because Gen X and Gen Y self-publish, we want to create ways for people to engage and participate as well as to be voyeurs. We continue to be surprised by the growth of the video-game industry as well as the spectrum of its fans. To capitalize on both its continued growth and its broadly based appeal, we are considering providing best-in-class venues where visitors can participate in their favorite genre of video gaming, whether it is, say, music, sports, or role-playing. The volume of visitors to Las Vegas provides fertile ground to establish such unique venues.

Our research into exclusivity and casino players' status boils down to a few things, one of which is that people love to be recognized in a resort or hotel—for example, by a concierge at the front desk. A second factor is that people prefer special VIP access. When Harrah's combines its loyalty-card system with a wireless digital infrastructure, visitors can be recognized, which can be translated into access. Today, we operate a less sophisticated version of that model.

We are masterful at using predictive modeling software to encourage visitors to do things they might not even plan on doing. We send out 300 million pieces of direct mail annually, and each one is customized to its recipient. We can send offers that will be compelling based on a visitor's past history. We will craft a visitor's experience so it meets his or her objective, but we are doing it for our own reasons. Tailoring advertisements to match the exhibited preferences of the guest provides a higher-value proposition so that he or she will stay and spend at Harrah's.

I don't know if Las Vegas is the most real place or the most unreal place in the world. There was a time when we talked about making it a family place, but that objective changed the day I became mayor. I didn't want it that way, and our advertisers didn't want it that way. Las Vegas is an adult playground, a place where people can fantasize. It is a real thing to be able to fantasize.
— Oscar Goodman

STUDIO ANALYSIS

Las Vegas Analysis The students were asked to make analysis drawings to look at specific issues that make the site unique and prepare to articulate the design problem. Each drawing isolates an idea, demonstrating how that issue operates within the area of investigation. When successful, these drawings identified themes during the design phase of the semester. For instance, one of these drawings offers a comparison between the grid of downtown Las Vegas, the "grid" of the Strip, and the grids of other cities, highlighting the fact that the Strip really has no grid; instead, it is a series of peculiar road networks attached to a central spine. This analysis resulted a stated goal; that is, if a pedestrian-friendly site is desirable, than a regular grid is needed. It also helps to explain something about the history of the Strip in contrast to downtown: as developers sought parcels to build resorts larger than the downtown grid would allow, they looked to the highway.

As described, analysis assignments can be fairly linear, sometimes even justifying design decisions after the fact. But in other instances, the analysis can be a process of discovery, akin to a scientific experiment whose results are as surprising as they are informative. The pedestrian circulation drawing fell into this category. While most of us had a hunch the sidewalks of Las Vegas were not regular and periodic (as they are in a city like New York), no one expected the results: the circulation plan looks like Tangier: nothing is linear or direct. Pedestrians may be required to double back or enter a building before bridging across the street. The figure/ground of the Strip is a series of spatially unique mousetraps, each resort devising a superior system for diverting the maximum volume of pedestrians into its shops and casinos. At Carnival Court, in front of Harrah's, Strip passersby are diverted deep into the property as the sidewalk wraps around an obstacle. Like the meandering shorelines of Scandinavia, Carnival Court increases its length of Strip frontage by shrewdly wrapping around a self-imposed obstacle. Drawing also revealed the interdependence between the public and private realms. In a traditional city grid, buildings front the sidewalk, and pedestrians can bypass any given lobby or commercial space. In Las Vegas, the sidewalk seamlessly becomes the shopping mall (as is the case at the Bellagio) or the gaming floor (as at the Flamingo). The relationship between traffic volume and profitability has given developers and designers a clear set of instructions, and the unstructured canvas of the Strip has provided ample room to experiment.

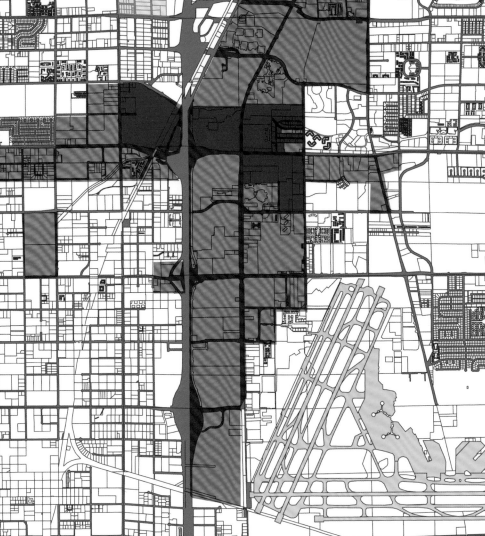

Las Vegas Region

The base map of this drawing is the state assessor's land plots for the metropolitan region of Las Vegas. Looking selectively at the plot densities, one can understand the densities characterizing Las Vegas. Major gaming areas are highlighted in pale pink and include the Strip, downtown, and east Las Vegas. Harrah's properties are highlighted in a vivid pink. The city limits of Las Vegas are indicated by the gray region to the north. Gaming and hospitality account for roughly 35 percent of employment.

Scale Comparison

The street grid of downtown Las Vegas and the Strip are contrasted with the grids of New York, Paris, and Rome. This illustrates the scale of Las Vegas's urban grid to cities commonly identified as "urban" and "walkable."

3/4 MILE SQUARE

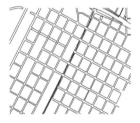

DOWNTOWN LAS VEGAS

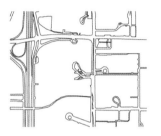

LAS VEGAS STRIP

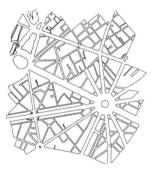

CENTRO, ROME

MIDTOWN NEW YORK CITY

SOHO, NEW YORK CITY

HAUSSMANN, PARIS

OLD PARIS

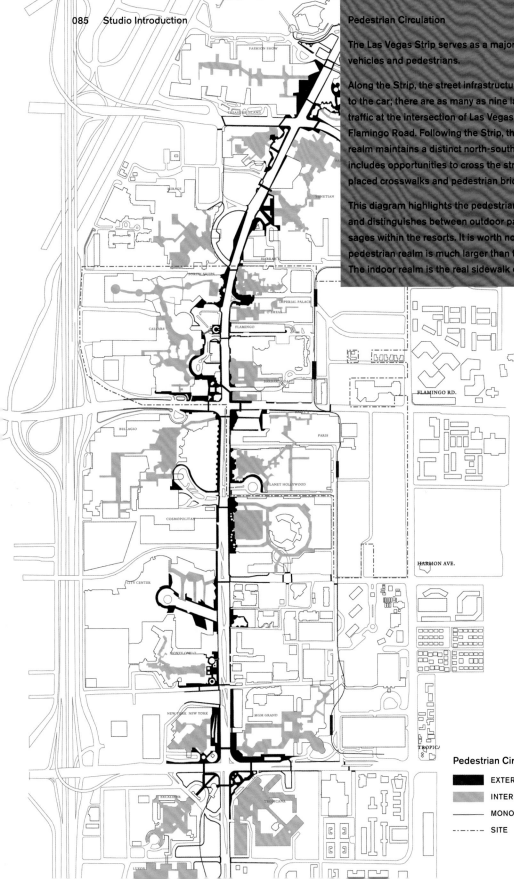

Pedestrian Circulation

The Las Vegas Strip serves as a major thoroughfare for vehicles and pedestrians.

Along the Strip, the street infrastructure gives preference to the car; there are as many as nine lanes of vehicular traffic at the intersection of Las Vegas Boulevard and Flamingo Road. Following the Strip, the pedestrian realm maintains a distinct north-south directionality, and includes opportunities to cross the street at sporadically placed crosswalks and pedestrian bridges.

This diagram highlights the pedestrian circulation network and distinguishes between outdoor paths and indoor passages within the resorts. It is worth noting that the indoor pedestrian realm is much larger than the outdoor realm. The indoor realm is the real sidewalk of Las Vegas.

FLAMINGO RD.

HARMON AVE.

Pedestrian Circulation

EXTERIOR CIRCULATION PATHS

INTERIOR CIRCULATION PATHS

MONORAIL

SITE

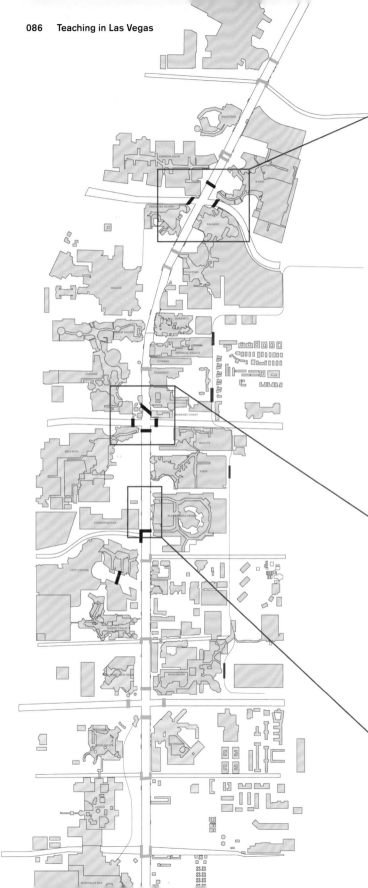

BRIDGE

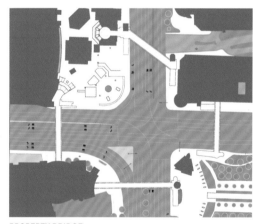

PROPERTY BRIDGE

AT-GRADE CROSSING

Vehicular Pedestrian Intersections

Illustration of the intersections between pedestrian paths and the street, highlighting the three principal crossing conditions:

1) The overhead bridge, necessitated by the expansion of the Strip and its intersecting streets to accommodate eight to ten lanes of traffic. Grade separation of vehicles and pedestrians has been adopted by Clark County as a way of reducing injuries and fatalities from collisions. Pedestrian bridges may lead to another sidewalk and sometimes empty directly onto the doorstep of a resort.

Due to the awkward placement of these bridges, pedestrians are forced to traverse much longer distances in order to get from one place to another. For instance, an 85-foot street crossing, between the Palazzo and Treasure Island resorts expands to a 1,650-foot, multibridge ordeal requiring nearly thirty minutes to navigate by foot.

2) The inter-resort bridge without connection to the sidewalk. This type of path does not allow for access to the sidewalk except via a route through the interior of a resort.

3) The street, or zebra, crossing. These at-grade crossings traverse up to ten lanes of traffic and leave the pedestrian exposed to the sun and aggressive drivers. Despite the lackluster options for exterior crossings, pedestrians in contemporary Las Vegas are asserting a strong desire to reclaim the outdoor sphere.

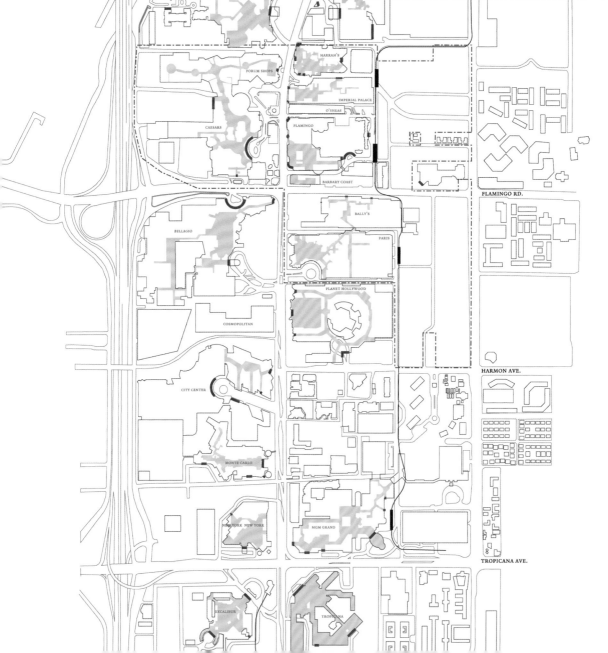

Resort Entries

This diagram highlights the entry portals to the resort interiors. There are invariably a number of entry points to each resort, some specializing in receiving vehicles or tour buses, others in welcoming VIPs or pedestrians, and many receiving a mixture thereof. Porte-cocheres are wide, multilane drop-off areas for cars and taxis and easily indentified by their characteristic semicircles; many porte-cocheres double as pedestrian entries, highlighting entrances that are favorable to vehicles. These entries often are pulled far back from the street to allow pedestrians rapid access to the resorts from Las Vegas Boulevard.

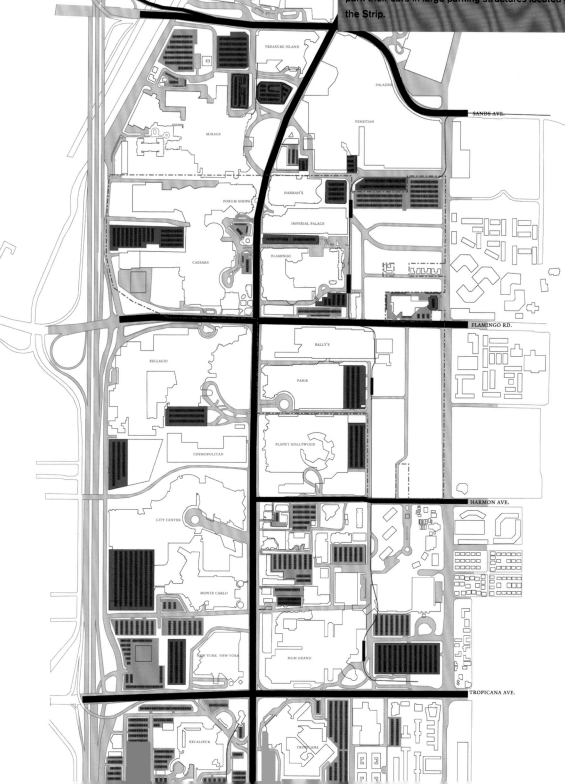

Parking

To park their vehicles, some guests hail a valet at porte-cochere entrances on Las Vegas Boulevard or park on a nearby side street. More budget-conscious guests can park their cars in large parking structures located off the Strip.

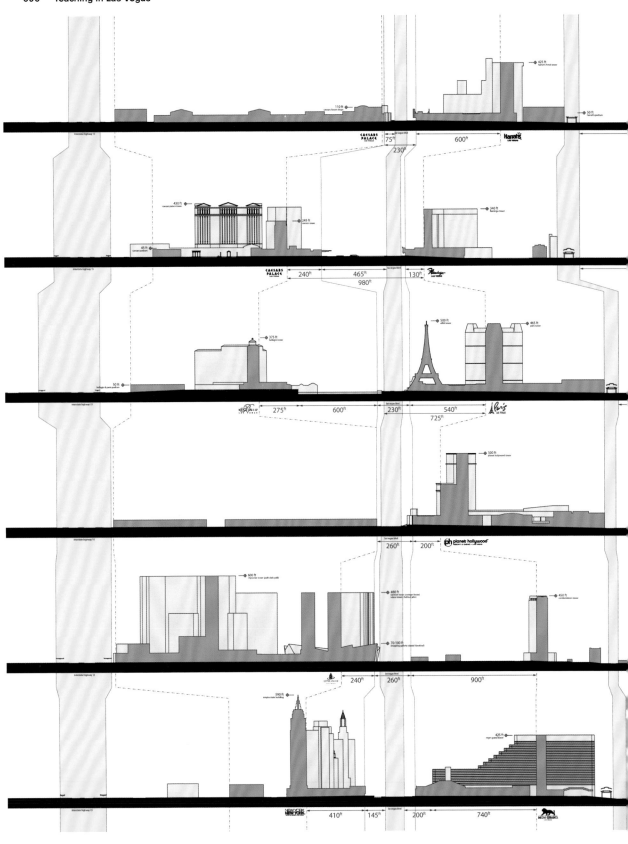

Strip Sections

An analysis of the transverse sectional relationships along the Strip reveals the scale of Las Vegas Boulevard by defining it in terms of metrics. Such metrics include a building's setback from the street, building-to-building distance, podium height, tower height, vehicular access, and sidewalk width.

Resort designs have changed over time, so the effect of different architectural ideas on the spatial quality of the Strip may be compared. For instance, an extreme example of the effect of setbacks on Las Vegas Boulevard becomes apparent when comparing the Bellagio, with its hotel tower framing a massive musical fountain spectacle, with the Flamingo, the towers of which are pushed right up to the street.

caesars forum shops - harrah's

caesars palace - flamingo

bellagio - paris

planet hollywood

city center - condominiums

new york new york - mgm grand

950ft

-18 ft

-18 ft
grade change

500 ft

Sections

LAS VEGAS STRIP

0 2 5   10   200   400

Key Plan

LAS VEGAS STRIP

0   ½ mile   1 mile

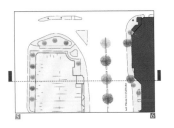

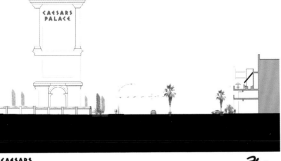

FASHION MALL

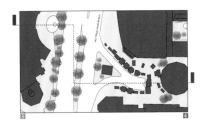

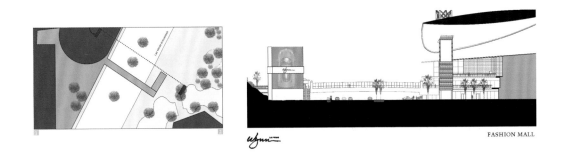

Detailed Sections

These drawings show various strategies to manipulate the sidewalk to pull pedestrians into the resorts along Las Vegas Boulevard. For example, at Fremont Street in downtown Las Vegas, the pedestrian path is central, and the buildings are close and open to the promenade. On the Strip, in front of Harrah's, there is a vehicular ramp that comes down and cuts off the pedestrian sidewalk, forcing visitors to come into the site and toward the resorts. In front of the Flamingo, the sidewalks are quite narrow. Similar to the Flamingo, Bill's Gamblin' Hall & Saloon is close to the sidewalk and open at the base so that the sidewalk spills right into the casino. The Bellagio employs a different strategy: it has a pedestrian bridge that empties directly into an indoor shopping area.

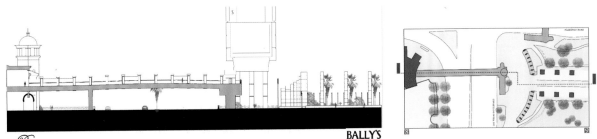

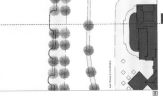

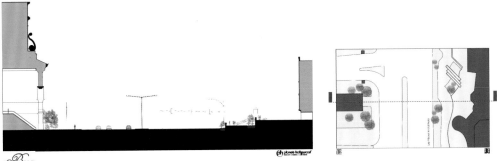

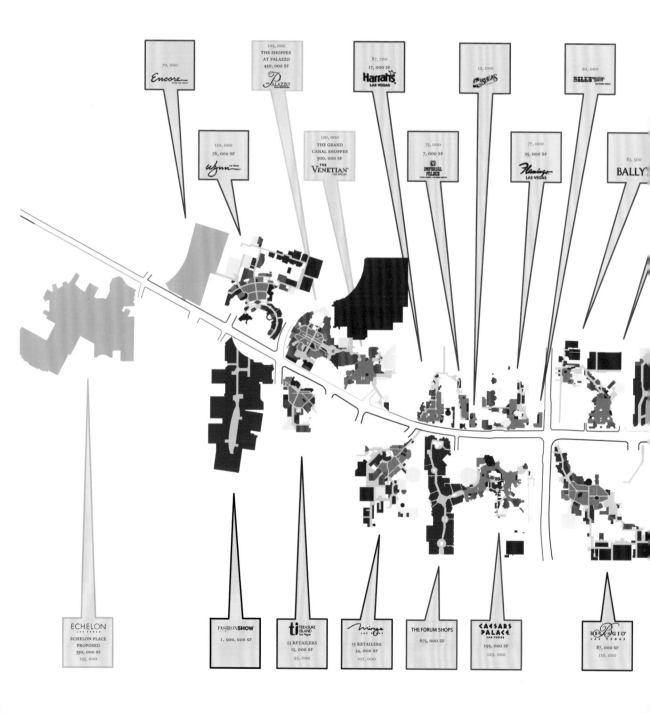

Land Use

This map shows the internal disposition of functions within resorts along the Strip. The square footage devoted to retail and gaming is indicated for each resort. For example, the plan of Caesars Palace shows the increased importance of retail in Las Vegas as the original casino floor is dwarfed by its newer retail appendage, the Forum Shops. The ownership of resorts is also indicated, demonstrating the growing conglomeration of individual properties into large mega-holdings.

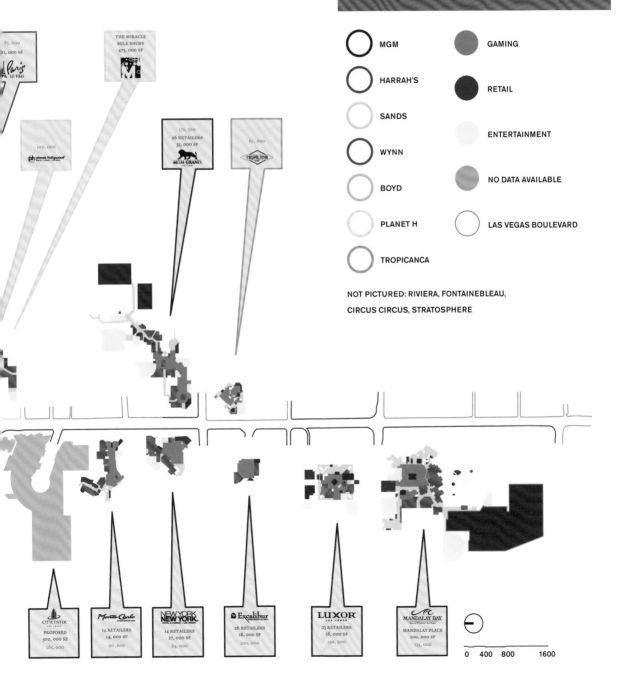

MGM

HARRAH'S

SANDS

WYNN

BOYD

PLANET H

TROPICANCA

GAMING

RETAIL

ENTERTAINMENT

NO DATA AVAILABLE

LAS VEGAS BOULEVARD

NOT PICTURED: RIVIERA, FONTAINEBLEAU,
CIRCUS CIRCUS, STRATOSPHERE

85,000
81,000 SF
Paris

THE MIRACLE
MILE SHOPS
475,000 SF

100,000
planet hollywood

171,500
26 RETAILERS
35,000 SF
MGM GRAND

61,000

CITYCENTER
PROPOSED
500,000 SF
165,000

Monte Carlo
14 RETAILERS
14,000 SF
90,000

NEW YORK
NEW YORK
14 RETAILERS
27,000 SF
84,000

Excalibur
26 RETAILERS
18,000 SF
100,000

LUXOR
23 RETAILERS
18,000 SF
120,000

MANDALAY BAY
MANDALAY PLACE
100,000 SF
135,000

0   400   800   1600

OWNER	MGM
STRIP MILES	2.66

RESORT	MGM GRAND	CITYCENTER	MANDALAY BAY	LUXOR	BELLAGIO	Mirage	Excalibur	TREASURE ISLAND	Monte Carlo	NEW YORK NEW YORK
GAMING	●	●	●	●	●	●	●	●	●	●
CASINO SF	171, 500	165, 000	135, 000	120, 000	116, 000	107, 000	100, 000	95, 000	90 ,000	84, 000
CASINO SF PER ROOM	34	34	36	27	39	35	25	33	30	40
HOTEL	■	■	■	■	■	■	■	■	■	■
ROOM KEYS	5, 034	4, 804	3, 700	4, 526	3, 005	3, 049	4, 032	2, 900	3, 014	2, 119
RDE OPTIONS PER 100 ROOMS	1	5	1	.8	2	2	.4	1.4	.8	1
RDE	54	250?	35	37	54	66	18	41	25	23
OPTIONS										

Resort Schedule

This schedule diagram of resorts allows for a comparison of resorts by several measures.

The information records the number of rooms, the size of casino, strip frontage (the length of the property along the Strip), RDE options (the number of separate retail, dining, and entertainment establishments), RDE options for each hotel room, and each casino's size in relation to its hotel rooms.

HARRAH'S						SANDS		WYNN	BOYD	PLANET H	TROPICANA
.91						.41		.39	.29	.23	.23
Harrah's	Paris	BALLY'S	Flamingo	IMPERIAL PALACE	BILL'S	THE VENETIAN	PALAZZO	Wynn / Encore	ECHELON	planet hollywood	TROPICANA
87,700	85,000	83,500	77,000	75,000	20,000	120,000	105,000	180,000	125,000	100,000	61,000
35	29	30	22	28	102	30	35	38	26	39	33
2,526	2,916	2,814	3,483	2,640	196	4,049	3,025	4,734	4,804	2,567	1,873
.7	1	1.5	.5	.8	3	3.1	4.1	1.6	5	7	.6
18	29	40	17	21	6	125	125	80	250?	185	11

Harrah's Campus: Pedestrian Routes

This drawing zooms in on the collection of resorts owned by Harrah's and highlights exterior and interior pedestrian routes; exterior space for the use of resort guests is shown, as well. Some of the most frequented pedestrian routes, such as the retail-lined "street" through the Forum Shops, are privately owned. There is often a greater continuity of paths within resorts than there is on the public street outside. The land-use attitude of Caesars differs from that of the Flamingo. The former creates an entry sequence for the car, while the latter pushes right up against the sidewalk, engulfing pedestrians in the sights, sounds, smells, and air-conditioning of the casino's interior.

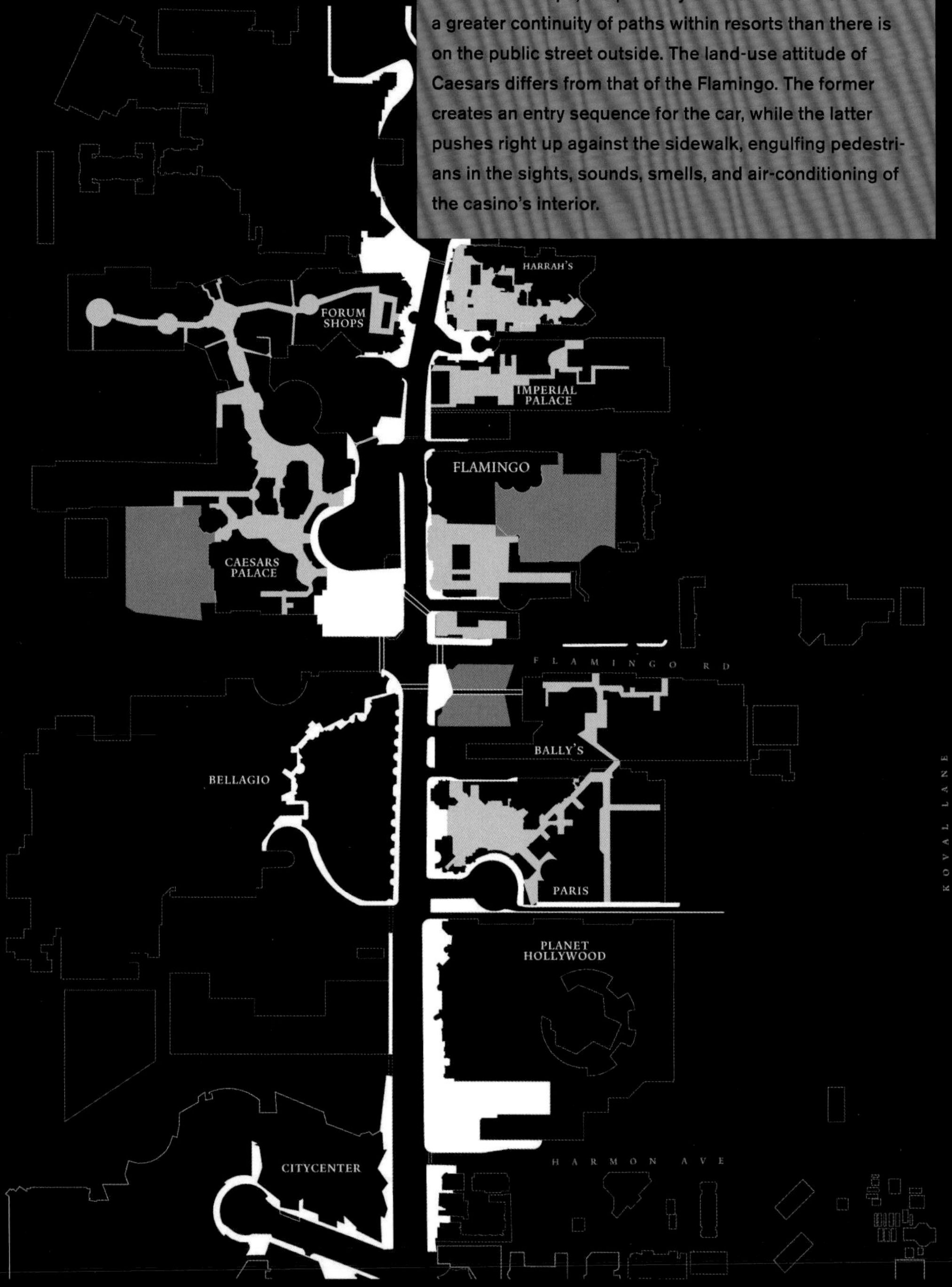

HARRAH'S

FORUM SHOPS

IMPERIAL PALACE

FLAMINGO

CAESARS PALACE

FLAMINGO RD

BALLY'S

BELLAGIO

PARIS

PLANET HOLLYWOOD

CITYCENTER

HARMON AVE

KOVAL LANE

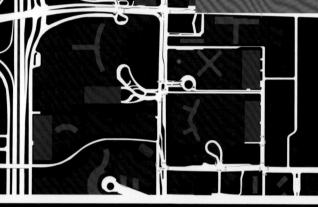

Top: Harrah's Campus: Vehicular Routes

This drawing shows the complex forms of the porte-cocheres on Harrah's campus. These vehicular entrances to the resorts must accommodate taxis, cars, and buses and often connect to valet parking lots. A density of parking structures around the resorts is necessary to hold employee and visitor cars. Unlucky guests may need to walk as far as a quarter-mile to reach their hotel room.

Bottom: Harrah's Campus: Pools and Green Space

This drawing shows the disposition of trees, plantings, pools, and water features around Harrah's resorts. The bulk of green and water space is reserved for the pool areas behind most resorts.

Las Vegas Downtown

Downtown Las Vegas and the Las Vegas Strip are entirely different experiences. Downtown Las Vegas is based on a grid system of streets, and the casino-resorts exist within that framework. Therefore, the resulting casinos are much smaller than the resorts on the Strip. They are oriented along one axis, Fremont Street. In an effort to reverse the district's decline, Fremont Street has been converted into a covered pedestrian promenade. The roof is fitted with LED screens that make it a giant, digital stage for the scheduled entertainment performances. Unlike the Strip, Fremont Street is tailored for the pedestrian, and every casino-resort along it follows a uniform, neon-lit street wall.

Intersection of Las Vegas Boulevard and Flamingo Road as seen from Caesars Palace.

III. LEARNING FROM LAS VEGAS

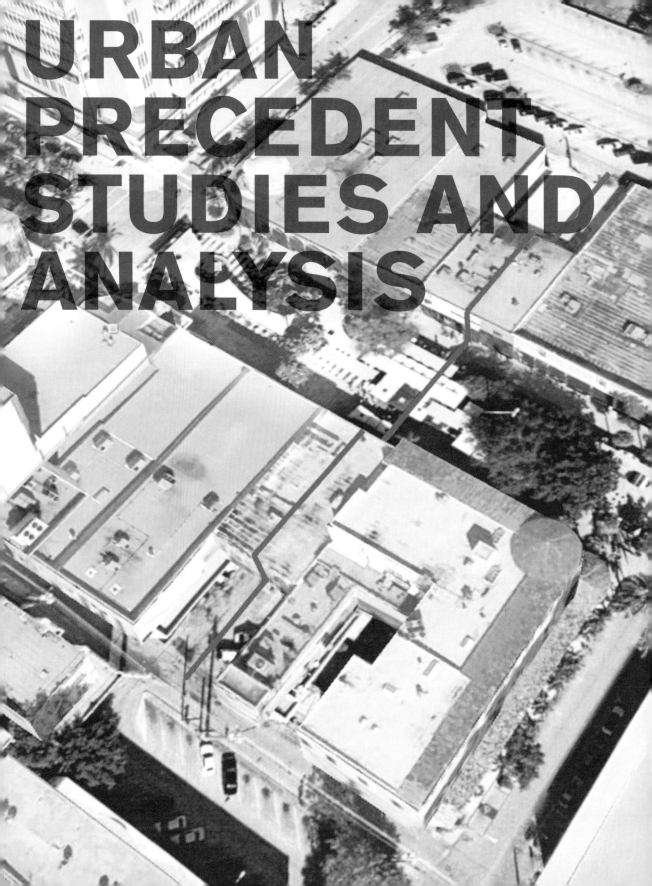

URBAN PRECEDENT STUDIES AND ANALYSIS

Learning from Elsewhere: Forty years ago, Denise Scott Brown and Robert Venturi led a Yale studio in Las Vegas to see what the world could learn from its "Main Street." This studio is founded on the opposite notion: Las Vegas needs to learn from the rest of the world. In the time since the first studio, Las Vegas has become a pedestrian environment, yet the city and its architecture have failed to respond to this trend. In spite of the lack of planned urbanism, millions of people walk in Las Vegas. As students pondered the future of the city, they needed to atone for its vehicular origins and imagine a place in which sidewalks make the journey from place to place enjoyable.

In preparation, we visited a number of successful environments. In Miami, we toured Morris Lapidus's 1960s renovation of Lincoln Road. Working with the existing city fabric, the street was closed to vehicular traffic and made into an exterior pedestrian mall, with shade to counter the heat and humidity of southern Florida. Within this pedestrian mall, Lapidus provided space for restaurants to turn inside out and offer seating areas mixed in with the plants, fountains, and follies. The result is a vibrant street where shoppers, diners, passersby, and tourists mix.

In Dallas we visited Victory, a large development that extends the gird of the downtown area onto formerly vacant land. The project is anchored by the American Airlines Center. In the years since its completion, numerous businesses and residences have filled out the area. A large hotel is across the street, and people walk. We also studied places we couldn't visit but are clearly ideal examples of successful pedestrian environments. Las Ramblas, in Barcelona, is a street made of four medieval streets linking the port to the newer city. Its medieval geometry gives the street a sense of surprise and delight, while small parks, courtyards, landscaped islands, and terraces contribute to a lush and comfortable environment attractive to pedestrians over the past few decades.

Lincoln Road Just a few blocks long, Miami's Lincoln Road epitomizes how dense landscaping, well-planned paths, and abundant outdoor seating can create a successful destination retail environment in which shoppers and pedestrians feel comfortable, even in the hot climate. Architect Morris Lapidus enlivens the 24-hour environment with street furniture, distinctive black-and-white-striped paving, shade from trees, and the weaving of the sidewalk between cafés and bars. In the eating and drinking establishments, water misters and umbrellas create micro-climates. Lincoln Road is rigorously calibrated, with special areas for street performers and vendors, both public and private outdoor seating areas, and a restrained building height compared with the towers that line the beachfront on either side of the retail street. Most visitors drive to Lincoln Road and park in adjacent lots, which isolates the road from the rest of the city.

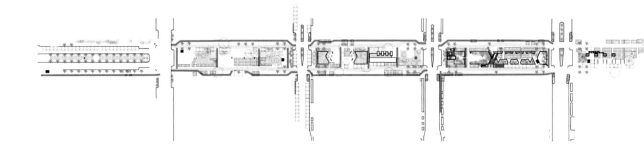

Lincoln Road

Top: Street section through Lincoln Road.
Bottom: Street level plan of Lincoln Road showing
trees, plants and vegetation.

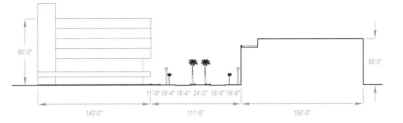

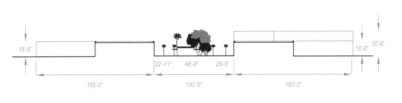

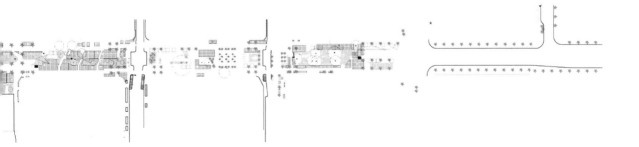

Las Ramblas Las Ramblas, in Barcelona, Spain, is a vital, pedestrian-oriented street. A large median strip forms the main pedestrian path down the center of the street, and narrow car lanes run parallel along its length. The tree canopy, cafés with terraces, and pavilions organize street life. Originating in the center of Barcelona at Plaza de Catalunya, Las Ramblas snakes its way three-quarters of a mile to the waterfront. Three subtle bends in the street divide the path into a sequence of four public spaces, each with a variety of courtyards that extend out laterally. The variation in the street's cross-section dimensions makes each point along its route unexpected and surprising.

Ramblas de Santa Monica

Las Ramblas

Connectivity analysis of intersections along Las Ramblas.

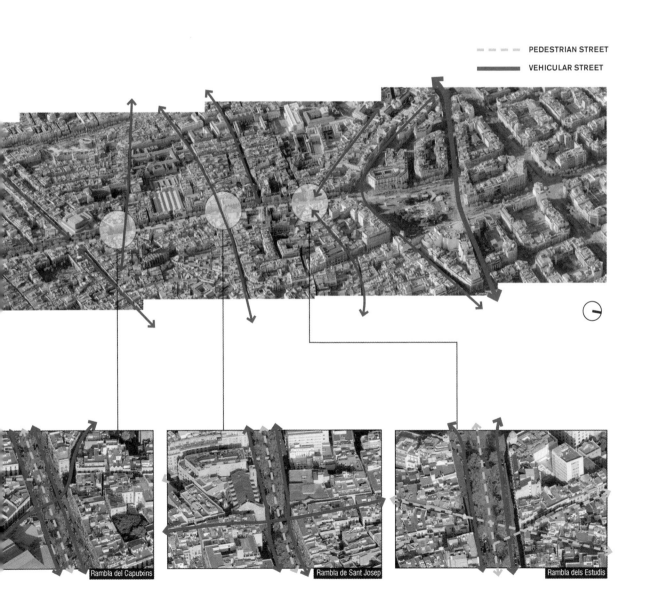

PEDESTRIAN STREET
VEHICULAR STREET

Rambla del Caputxins

Rambla de Sant Josep

Rambla dels Estudis

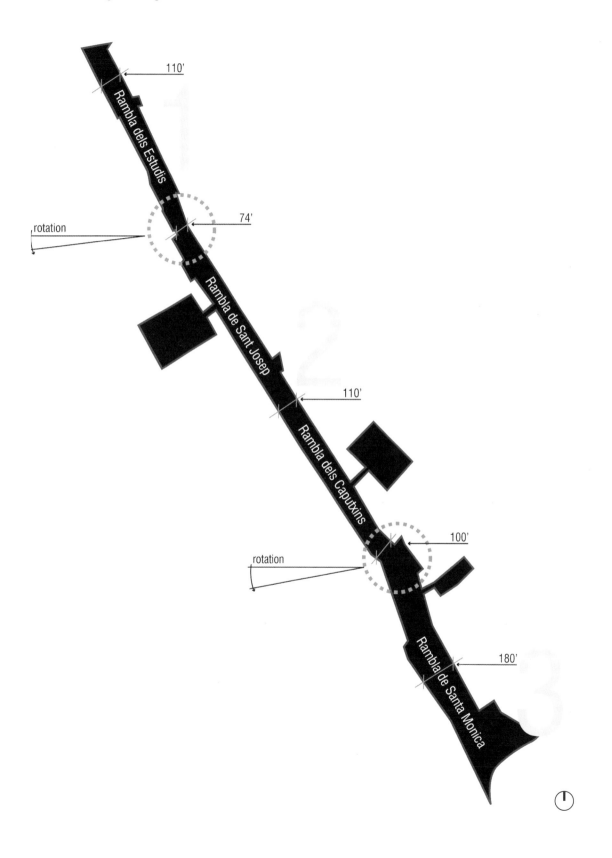

Las Ramblas

Sections along the length of Las Ramblas show the
sectional variety of the street.
Opposite: Diagram showing the four medieval streets
joined to make Las Ramblas. The inflections create
distinct spatial zones.

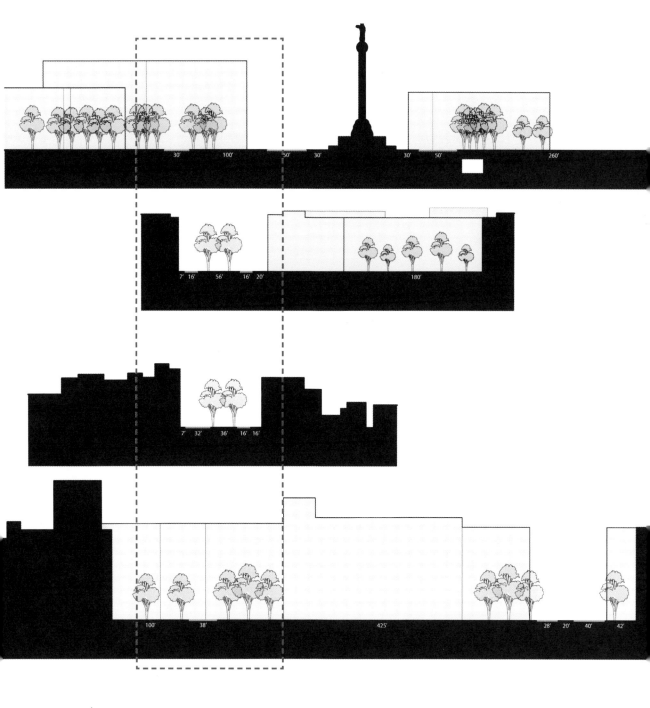

Third Street Promenade The Third Street Promenade, in Santa Monica, California, is considered one of the premier shopping destinations in west Los Angeles for residents and tourists alike. It has been a center of business since the town's founding in the late 1800s. In the 1960s, the Santa Monica Mall jump-started the development of the promenade. In 1984, the city of Santa Monica founded the Third Street Development Corporation to reinvigorate the promenade, which terminates at Santa Monica Place, a mall on the south end designed by Frank Gehry in 1980. Today, a variety of street performers entertain pedestrians at various intervals along the street, creating vital urban activity and attractions.

Third Street Promenade

Tenant mix along Third Street Promenade.

RESTAURANT   OFFICE   PARKING GARAGE

CAFÉ   THEATER   - - - STUDY AREA

RETAIL   RESTROOMS

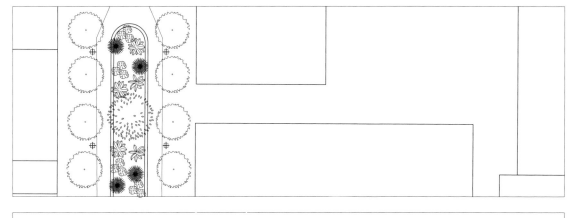

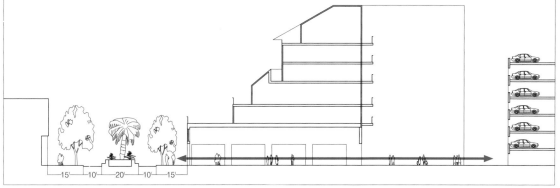

15'   10'   20'   10'   15'

A

Third Street Promenade

Top: Public seating is oriented to look down the length of the street.
Bottom: Building height limits ensure plenty of light and fresh air along the promenade.
Opposite: Public seating is oriented to encourage pedestrian movement across the street, from storefront to storefront.

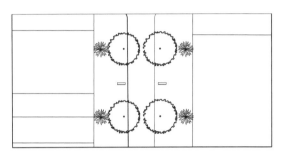

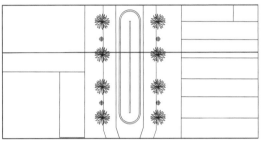

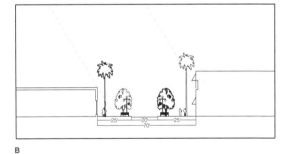

B

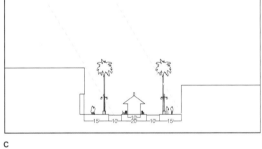

C

Bleecker Street Bleecker Street, in New York City, runs from Greenwich Village on the lower West Side to NoHo— or north of Houston—on the Lower East Side as it samples a number of neighborhoods along its path. The city's famed music venues draw people to the street as do retail spaces on the ground floor of the historic brownstone residences. At Eighth Avenue, the street has a more residential character, while toward Laguardia Place and the neighboring New York University campus, it has a more entertainment-geared atmosphere. This transition is reflected in the varying setbacks of the buildings and sidewalk width as well as in the bicycle lanes and landscaping.

Bleecker Street

Diagram showing ground-level uses on Bleecker Street.

RESIDENTIAL/HOTEL
RETAIL
PUBLIC SCHOOL K–6
PAROCHIAL SCHOOL
RELIGIOUS INSTITUTIONS

BOWERY HOTEL

MERCER HOTEL

City Place City Place, in West Palm Beach, Florida, is a mixed-use development that is perpendicular to downtown's Clematis Street. However, bounded by rail lines to the east, an eight-lane highway to the south, and an institutional development to the west, City Place effectively has been isolated from the context of West Palm Beach; intended as a way to duplicate Clematis Street's success in attracting visitors to the downtown area, the development has shifted the commercial program away from downtown. Circular ambulatory routes and radiating programmatic hier-archies concentrate activity in the exterior plaza at the heart of City Place and away from the street front. As a series of programmed spaces, it is organized as a public plaza wrapped by commercial development, townhouses, and apartment buildings. Parking decks are hidden between the commercial and residential spaces. Clever orientation and pathways seamlessly lead pedestrians through upper-level and ground-floor retail. An existing church and plaza have been transformed into an open-air restaurant that is encircled by an arched pedestrian promenade, creating a stage-like effect that both dramatizes the plaza and attracts spectators to the second-level retail and dining establishments. Most of City Place's circulation is on the exterior, but it is shaded by trees and cooled with fans and water misters. The development resolves the problem of externalizing a shopping environment in a hot, humid climate and represents a well-designed prototype for a mixed-use urban revitalization development project.

City Place

City Place in context.

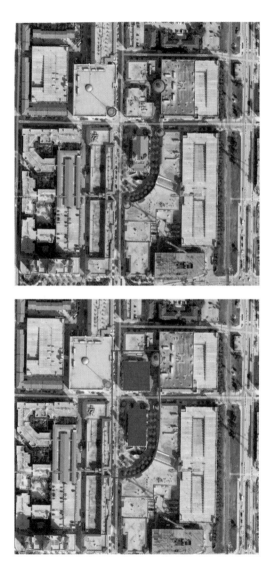

City Place

Section through plaza next to the Harriet Himmel Theatre.
Opposite: Rotunda entry points to interior.

Seaside Seaside Florida, planned by Andrés Duany and Elizabeth Plater-Zyberk, shows how prioritizing walkability can enhance the property values of a community. With its careful metrics and specific building requirements, the planned neighborhood became a prototype for New Urbanism. However, it is often critiqued as a vacation resort masquerading as a town. Through its zoning and code guidelines—which set standard town land policies for everything from picket fences, paint color, setbacks, and side yards—Seaside is maintained as a quaint village with distinctive public spaces.

The real strength of the development is how the public space is oriented toward the main amenities of the Florida coast: everything is arranged to share the beach, sea, and sun. Typical waterfront developments privatize the beach-front, dividing the shoreline into lots that are disconnected from one another. Seaside orients the town's main green space and radial street pattern toward the public beach and water views.

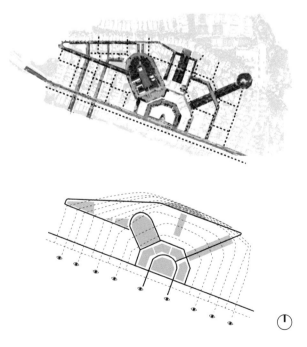

Seaside

Top to Bottom: Typical proportions for a large street, an avenue, a small street, and a footpath.
Opposite: Seaside street network and green spaces.

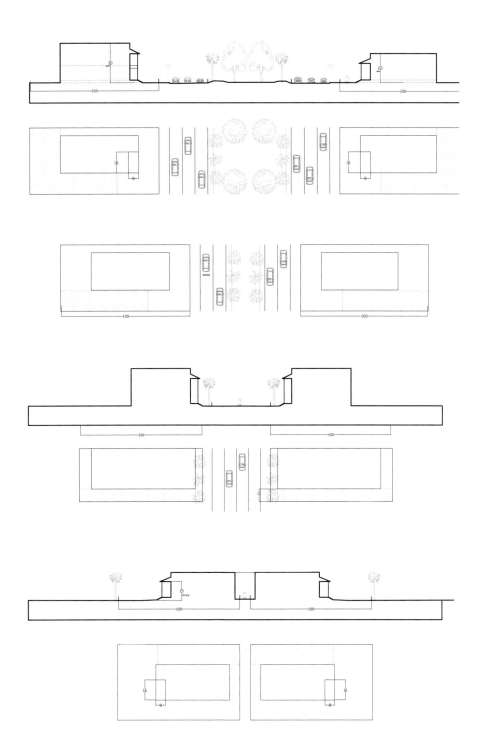

Victory A mixed-use development just outside of downtown Dallas, Texas, Victory has the American Airlines Arena as its principal anchor, infusing the district with thousands of visitors before, during, and after a concert or game. Conceived as a way to span a hole in the urban fabric, the master plan defines a grid that connects to the edge of the downtown street grid, providing more circulation for traffic. While the arena preceded much of the development, thoughtful planning foresaw that the development parcels would become desirable as the success of the arena began to radiate outward. Today, much of that prospecting has come to fruition, evidenced by streets dotted with shops, bars, and retail spaces. Recently added residential space and a W Hotel have transformed the area into a large-scale mixed-use urban project. For instance, a public plaza fronting the arena is flanked by mixed program, including a studio that broadcasts a morning TV show.

While the city's love of cars remains firmly ingrained, the project has successfully has embedded a new model that favors walkable streets, mixed uses, and urban density. The master plan's real coup is to expand the downtown area by connecting it to the city's grid.

Victory

Section through Victory showing plaza proportions.

NEW
LAS VEGAS
MASTER
PLAN

TREASURE ISLAND

MIRAGE

VENETIAN

SANDS EXPO

SHOW MALL

S. HIGHLAND DR.

CAESARS PALACE

HARRAH'S

13.05 ACRES

4.80 ACRES

9.84 ACRES

IMPERIAL PALACE

8.60 ACRES

EAST SIDE

31.06 ACRES

FLAMINGO

1.79 ACRES

85.53 ACRES

80.11 ACRES

25.19 ACRES

WESTIN CASUARINA

2.34 ACRES

BARBARY COAST

4.20 ACRES

1.19 ACRES

2.66 ACRES

6.93 ACRES

BELLAGIO

BALLY'S

29.92 ACRES

PARIS

23.91 ACRES

12.80 ACRES

COSMOPOLITAN

ALADDIN

CITY CENTER

14.10 ACRES

1.62 ACRES

11.54 ACRES

PANORAMA

POLO TOWERS

MONTE CARLO

S. LAS VEGAS BLVD.

MARTIN LUTHER KING BLVD.

WILD WILD WEST

NEW YORK NEW YORK

MGM

Harrah's Campus Master Plan The studio's program and site were selected to provoke the post-suburban condition of twenty-first-century Las Vegas. The studio focused on one of Las Vegas's most trafficked spots, at the intersection of Flamingo Road and the Strip, where Harrah's owns seven adjacent resorts. The site also includes dozens of acres of recently acquired land between the existing Las Vegas Boulevard resorts and Koval Lane to the east. The studio program incorporated several adjacent parcels, each with a large casino and several thousand hotel rooms. What we now think of as the Harrah's campus was assembled only recently under a single proprietorship. Initially, each project was conceived as an independent entity; the studio challenged the students to conceive of the pieces as components of a single master plan. Stemming from their earlier analysis of the 270-acre campus, each two-student team was asked to develop a strategy for the campus's future development, merging an architectural precedent from their earlier assignments with their goals for the Harrah's site. The basic program given to the students included an arena, two new casino-resorts, a significant retail, dining, and entertainment expansion as well as boutique hotels, meeting space, and office space.

Back-of-Strip parcels were included, extending focus from the Strip to other major Las Vegas arterial roads. For some students, these parcels were a starting point for rethinking the development patterns that have characterized Las Vegas and post–World War Two America. The master-plan designs pushed each team to clarify and define its attitude toward the site, preparing the students to make the next series of decisions for the building-design portion of the semester.

New Strips on the Strip: Terry Chew, Nicholas Hanna, Lauren Mishkind and Christopher Starkey Despite the Strip's history as a roadside attraction, contemporary Las Vegas is clearly a pedestrian experience. Our master plan takes advantage of the extraordinary pedestrian load on the Strip by improving the inadequate provisions for foot traffic and inserting a series of new pedestrian promenades connecting Harrah's existing casinos. Since the majority of visitors walk between destinations, this proposal aims to create a desirable pedestrian environment so that visitors naturally spend more time and money on the Harrah's campus. Retail, dining, and entertainment venues animate both sides of these new promenades and are serviced from the existing back-of-house facilities in the casinos. The project inserts a new north-south pedestrian street, halving the existing half-mile street grid to make an environment on an urban scale and providing frontage to accommodate the new program as an outdoor pedestrian streetscape. The natural topography to the west of the Strip meant our master plan could service the new casino resorts and hotels underneath the pedestrian level by keeping the promenades at the Strip's elevation. One result of this strategy is the addition of a significant parking area, which did not require expensive excavation into the hard Las Vegas soil.

The underlying challenge of the master plan was to fortify Harrah's competitive position on the Strip by encouraging visitors to spend more time at the casino properties than at its competitors. The capture-and-sequester design strategy draws customers by waylaying them deep within Harrah's labyrinthine interior. Since Harrah's has such a large, contiguous piece of land, the building design plan could create an open and clearly navigable network of attractions.

At portal points between Harrah's and its competitors, the proposal uses passive strategies to create "one way" entries, that are nevertheless visually open. Drawing from urban precedents, we adopted both desirable as well as unpleasant qualities—such as annoying noises and the tactical removal of shade—to compel the visitor to move toward Harrah's.

New Strips on the Strip

Master plan for Harrah's showing alterations to existing buildings and proposed new construction.

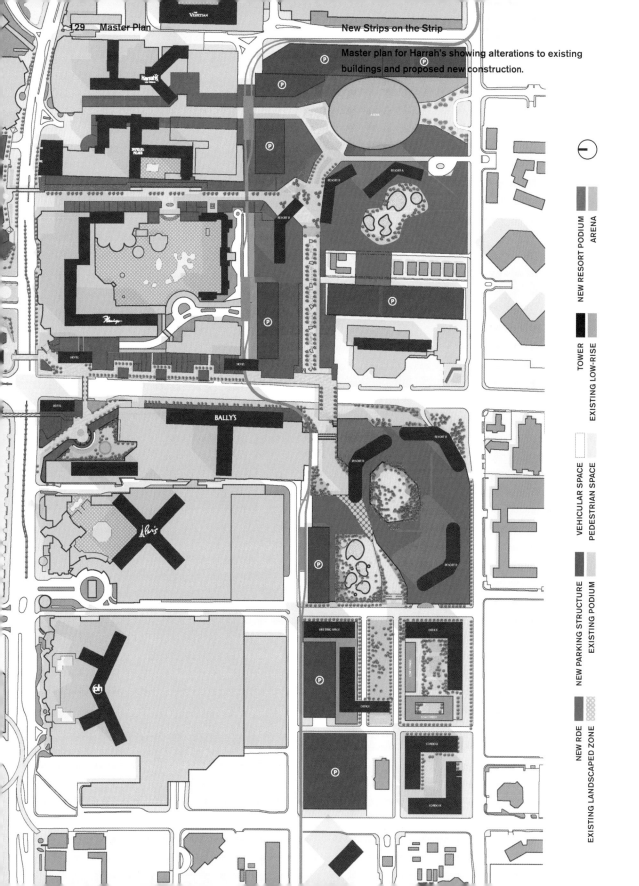

NEW RDE

NEW PARKING STRUCTURE

VEHICULAR SPACE

TOWER

NEW RESORT PODIUM

EXISTING LANDSCAPED ZONE

EXISTING PODIUM

PEDESTRIAN SPACE

EXISTING LOW-RISE

ARENA

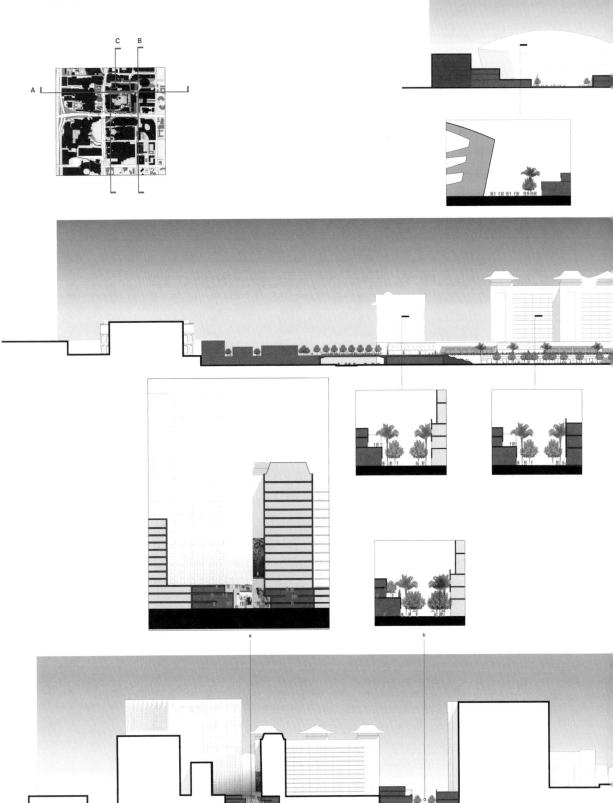

New Strips on the Strip

Sections showing streetscape of proposed pedestrian
passages between and behind existing Harrah's resorts
on Las Vegas Boulevard.

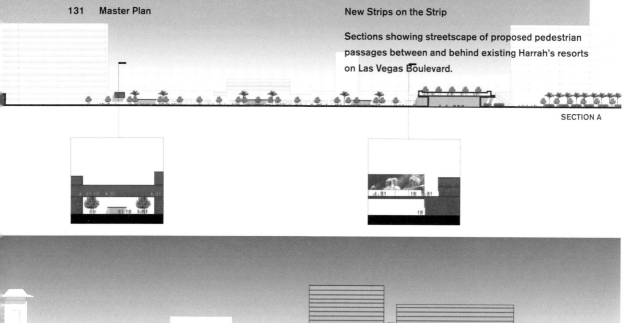

SECTION A

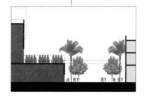

SECTION B

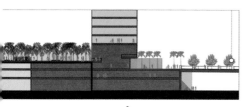

SECTION C

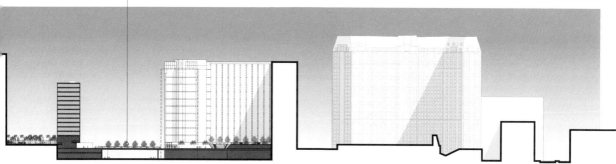

La Via

Opposite top: Existing and proposed pedestrian circulation
paths, building massing, and public spaces.
Opposite bottom: Master plan for Harrah's campus
showing alterations in front of Caesars Palace, a new
pedestrian path between the Flamingo and Imperial
Palace, and new construction.

La Via: Eric Krancevic, Louise Levi, and Tom Tang Environments that draw a crowd are good for business. For most commercial enterprises, potential customers are drawn in from the streets, but in Las Vegas some of the most vital pedestrian thoroughfares are interior environments. Our proposal, La Via, makes a nod to interior streetscapes that successfully create a vibrant environment for commerce, such as the Forum Shops or the lamp-lit "boulevards" in the Paris resort. Our scheme aims to strengthen Harrah's existing revenue model of casinos and hotels by linking its properties with a 24-hour, mixed-use pedestrian boulevard offering retail, entertainment, and dining on the street and on balconies; office space is on the upper floors. The exterior space, scaled to the pedestrian, is a continuation of Las Vegas Boulevard's grade and connects to the interior "street" at multiple points throughout Harrah's campus.

Our second idea is to add a sequence of features at a monumental scale, similar to the Bellagio fountain. The first feature is a public plaza in front of the proposed arena, which is activated by convention-goers during the day and by visitors to the arena at night. This public feature is complemented on the south side of the property by a spectacle called the Beach. Whereas the Bellagio has only one thousand rooms facing its fountain, our plan gives Harrah's two thousand rooms with views of the Beach—more eyes make the Beach more of a spectacle. Further, whereas the Bellagio's fountain is placed on the Strip, the Beach spectacle is internalized by the plan, surrounded by the resort's profitable program of restaurants, bars, entertainment, and retail spaces. This distinct space creates beachfront views for our two new resorts by activating the resort's southern parcels. Another 24-hour environment with segmented offerings sells different levels of exclusivity—boat rentals, private cabanas, floating pools, lounge chairs at the water's edge—during the day. At night, clubs and movie projections create an entertainment-filled, star-lit experience.

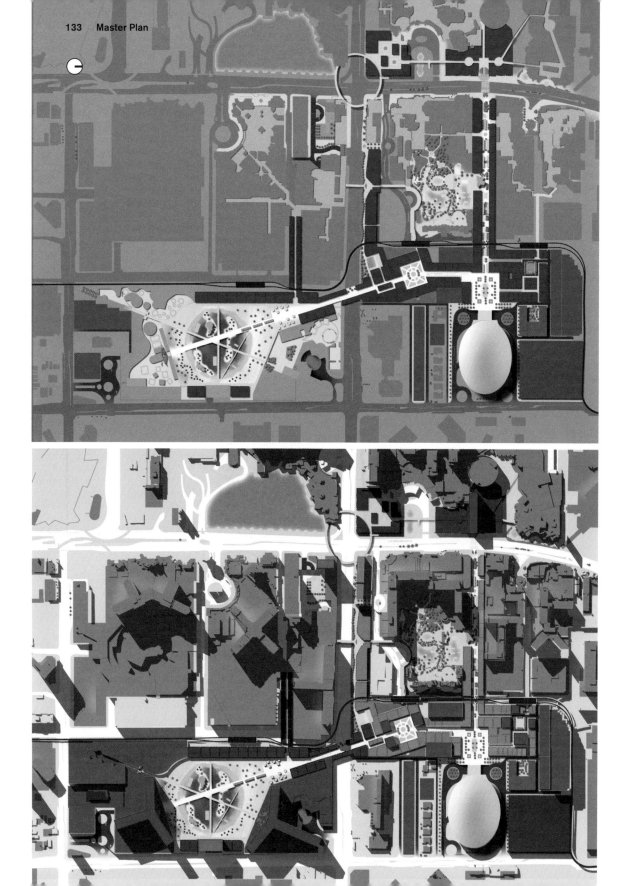

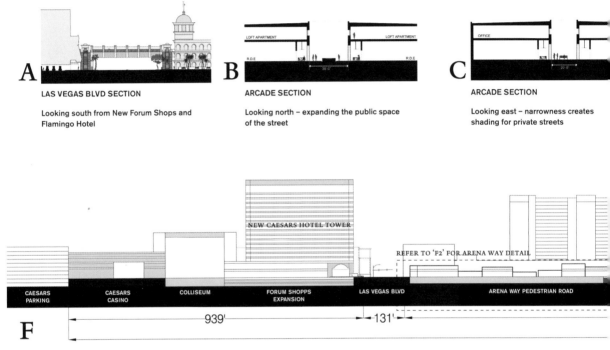

A

LAS VEGAS BLVD SECTION

Looking south from New Forum Shops and
Flamingo Hotel

B

ARCADE SECTION

Looking north – expanding the public space
of the street

C

ARCADE SECTION

Looking east – narrowness creates
shading for private streets

F

HARRAH'S CAMPUS SITE SECTION

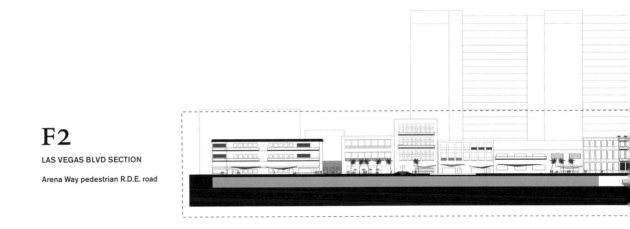

F2

LAS VEGAS BLVD SECTION

Arena Way pedestrian R.D.E. road

Sections showing streetscape of proposed streets.

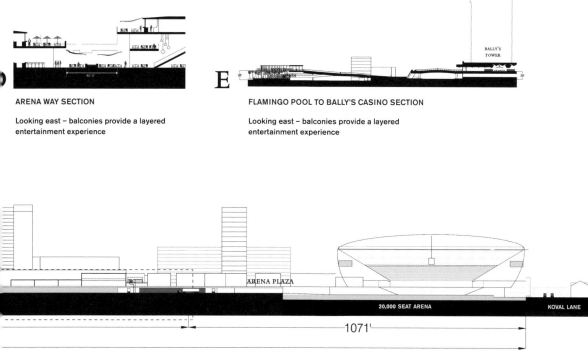

ARENA WAY SECTION

Looking east – balconies provide a layered
entertainment experience

FLAMINGO POOL TO BALLY'S CASINO SECTION

Looking east – balconies provide a layered
entertainment experience

ARENA PLAZA

20,000 SEAT ARENA   KOVAL LANE

1071'

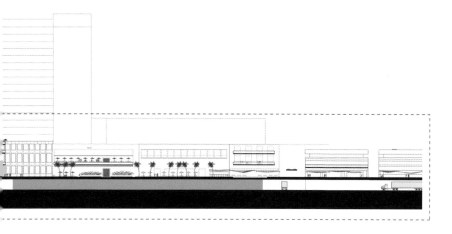

The Strip Reconsidered, Expansion East: Zakery Snider, Cheng-Hui Chua, and Patrick McGowan The development of Las Vegas has happened backward. What is now the Strip was a thinly populated highway fifty years ago. Subsequent development continued to add density, and eventually something resembling a city grid grew from the Strip. But the planning and foresight that typically precedes a city plan were never allowed to happen. Instead, a cumulative series of patches and short-term solutions have been applied. Our master plan attempts to undo the accumulated growth by applying urban standards to Harrah's campus.

Cities become famous for their neighborhoods. Our scheme segments Harrah's campus into three different neighborhoods by proposing new streets that connect the existing resorts to new development parcels. One neighborhood is a luxury boulevard anchored by Caesars Palace and the Forum Shops at one end and a new luxury resort at the other. The second neighborhood is anchored by the new arena, located on Flamingo Road. This existing street is the most populous, and we take advantage of the existing density of pedestrian traffic on what is commonly thought of as the center of the Strip. The third neighborhood is populated by hip clubs and edgy dive bars. Its main street is wedged into a narrow slot of space, and the overall feel is a counterpoint to the luxury boulevard.

In the shadow of Harrah's campus, the CityCenter resort is nearing completion. MGM's concept is to make a single resort with the density and offerings of a city. We propose the opposite, instead making the Harrah's campus itself a city of strategically themed streets connecting all of Harrah's current and future resorts. This strategy recognizes that people like to wander from resort to resort rather than stay in one place. By organizing the campus into neighborhoods, future development can happen in a flexible manner, paralleling the development patterns of authentically generated cities.

The Strip Reconsidered, Expansion East

Roof plan of new master plan for Harrah's campus. A main
feature of this proposal is the stadium, which straddles
Flamingo Road mid block.

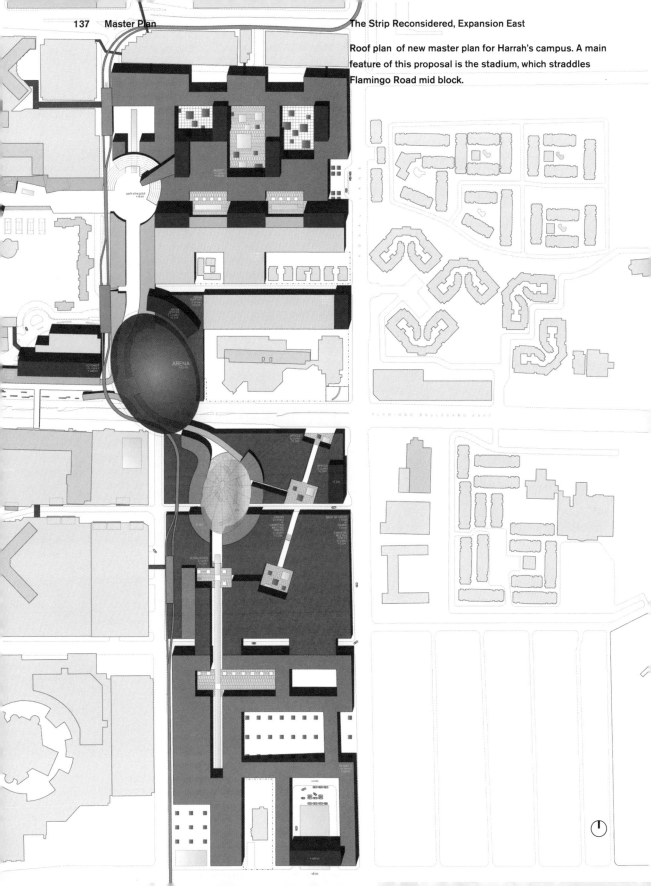

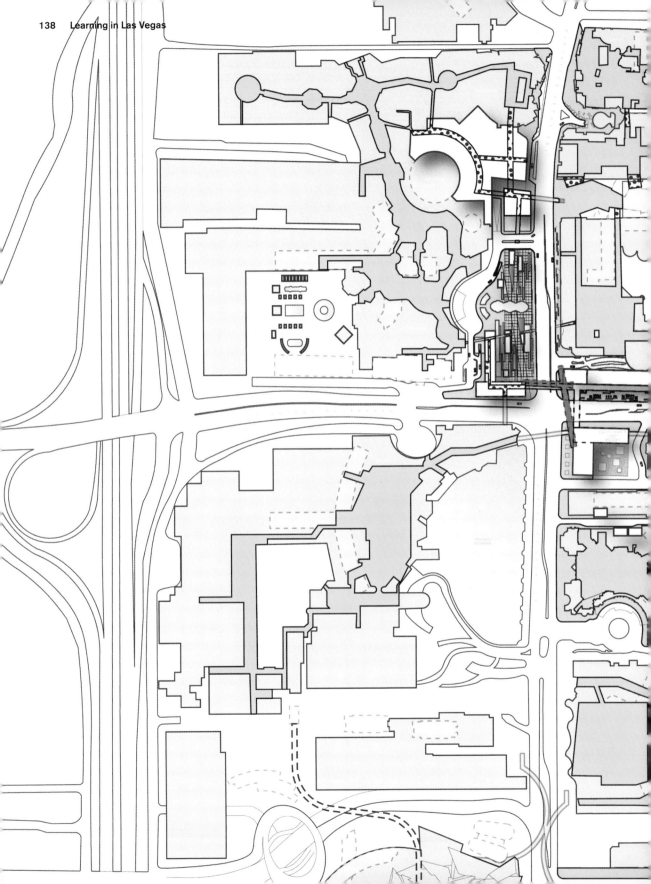

The Strip Reconsidered, Expansion East

Pedestrian plan of proposal for Harrah's campus.
Exterior and interior pedestrian routes are highlighted
in yellow.

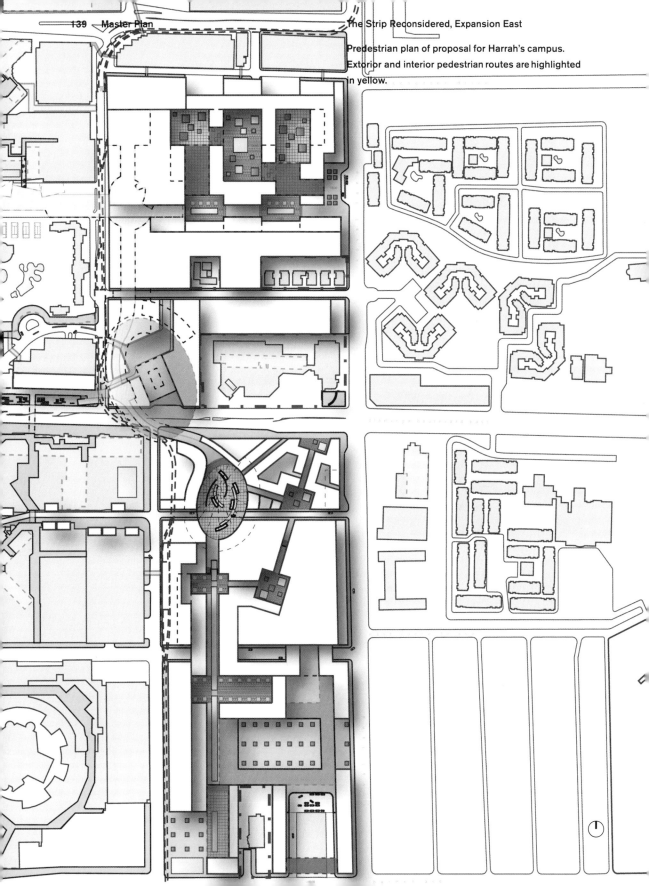

Plan highlighting vehicular routes around master plan
proposal for Harrah's campus.

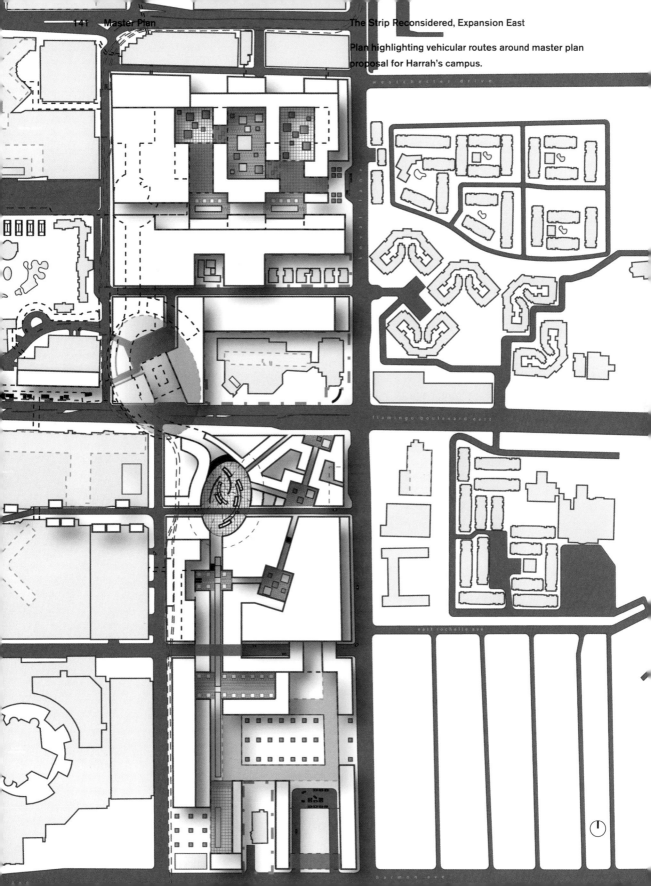

NEW RESORTS

Building Designs Students worked in teams of two and selected from their master plans a parcel to develop in greater detail as a building design. Building development was presented as a two-prong proposition: it needed to reinforce the concepts of the master plan while demonstrating an understanding of the program type and selected location. The inherent issues in each team's selection set up their building investigation and augmented their master-planning work. While each team was allowed to develop its own program according to the type selected, the team worked closely with developer Charles Atwood to make its proposals more believable, absorbing his concerns and ideas during the design process. Ultimately, each team had different attitudes toward the site and ended up with vastly different building approaches and sizes.

Before deciding on a building for further development, the students had to convince Atwood that their ideas were consistent with Harrah's business plan. A proposal to add yet another mega resort had to be balanced with overall economic goals. One proposal strategically located a boutique hotel on a site too small for a normal sized hotel. The particular hotel demographic reinforced the master plan, supporting arguments to attract customers Harrah's is currently underserving. Another team looked into the future when a new full-scale resort would be desirable, but Strip-front land wouldn't be available. Their master plan proposed a free-standing resort connected to the Strip by a to-be-developed street.

Eventually, the students' ideas were tested by a final jury, including two private-equity directors who co-own Harrah's, as well as the casino's director of development. Each project's assumptions and direction were questioned, and the students had to make decisions that would stand up to professional scrutiny.

Enclave: Tom Tang and Patrick McGowan The Enclave resort is a mixed-use project located at the busiest intersection in Las Vegas. It revels in the joy of activity and excitement by seamlessly integrating retail, dining, and entertainment program with pedestrian and vehicular infrastructure. Towering above the public realm is a slim tower of hotel rooms. Our scheme connects the public spaces to the adjacent street corners with a "social ring," a pedestrian path integrated with the commercial venues. The spaces are programmed and branded to siphon off passersby both young and trendy, which is Harrah's target demographic for this area of its campus. An outdoor theater cantilevers over Las Vegas Boulevard, marking the project with an iconic form. The solution is meant to leverage Harrah's most valuable property by adding program at the most heavily trafficked place on Harrah's campus. At the same time, it represents the next generation of Clark County's trend to separate pedestrians from vehicles at busy Strip intersections. Rather than simply providing a bridge across the main street, the outdoor theater becomes a revenue-generating space and a front door to Harrah's campus.

Enclave

Night rendering of the Enclave.

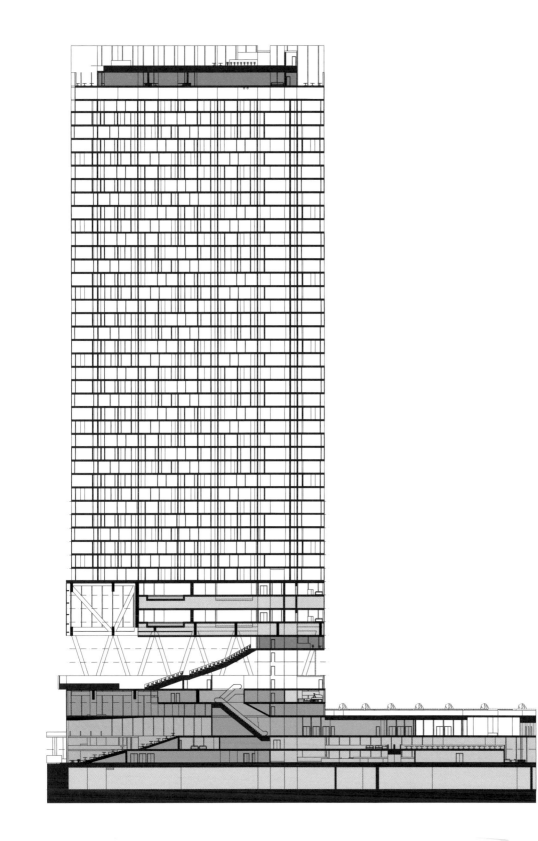

Enclave

Typical floor plan in tower.
Opposite: Longitudinal section through the Enclave resort.

Enclave

Presentation model.

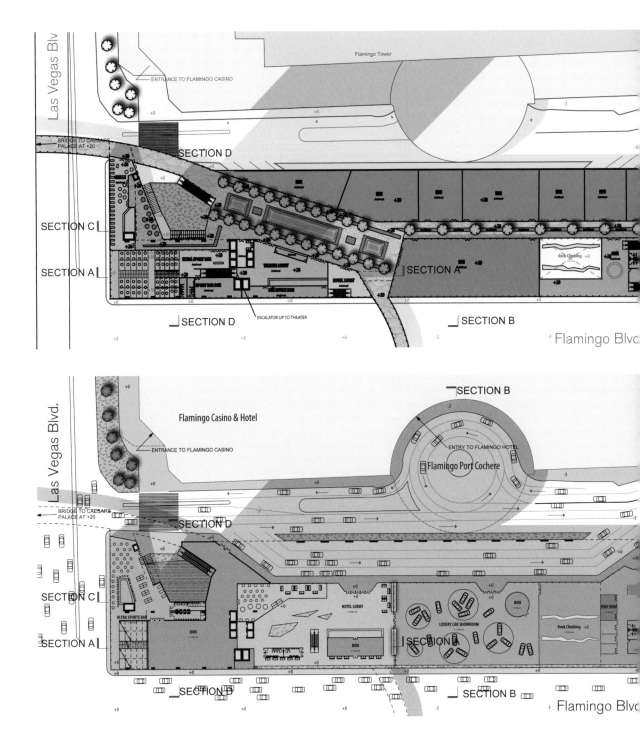

Enclave

Top: Promenade-level plan showing connection to the
circulation "ring."
Bottom: Ground-floor plan.

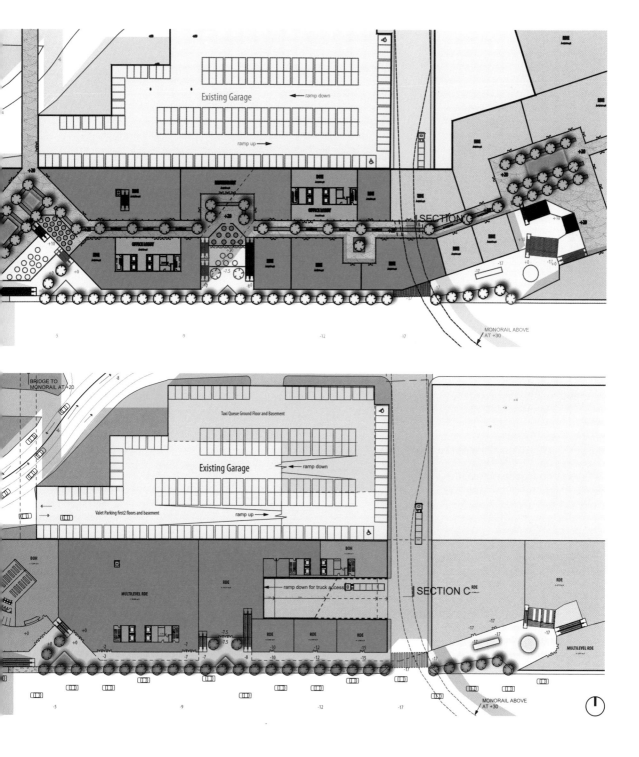

The Woods: Nicholas Hanna and Christopher Starkey In the well-established Steve Wynn design typology, a colossal, attention-grabbing spectacle should front a property—for example, the volcano at The Mirage, the pirate show at Treasure Island, and the dancing fountains at the Bellagio. However, this mainstay of Las Vegas's architectural logic has its downsides. For example, a spectacle can grow stale, making the public search for another mecca in which to spend their money. Also, as it is traditionally designed, the large-scale spectacle not only renders unoccupiable a large swath of land but pushes the resort back from the street, further thwarting potential visitors. The Woods, our proposed 2,500-room casino-resort that sits off the Strip, reorganizes the Wynn paradigm by making occupiable the space around the spectacle.

The center of the Woods resort is an animated and visually frenetic plaza that doubles as the nexus of three pedestrian paths. Three hotel towers surround the plaza, which is edged with retail, dining, and entertainment venues. By concentrating foot traffic, our scheme surrounds the much-vaunted spectacle with a spectacle that never grows old: people-watching.

The plaza is above the existing grade, allowing for the insertion of the casino under the plaza. Perforations in the plaza connect the two levels. A dramatic, eight-story velvet curtain in front of the main hotel tower leads the plaza's visitors down a grand staircase into the casino, which is the beating heart of the building's circulation, linking together all the functions of the resort from check-in and elevator cores to the spa's pool. In turn, this "racetrack" loop is ringed by more retail and dining venues. At the site's perimeter, the back-of-house and loading-dock spaces are all underground and out of sight.

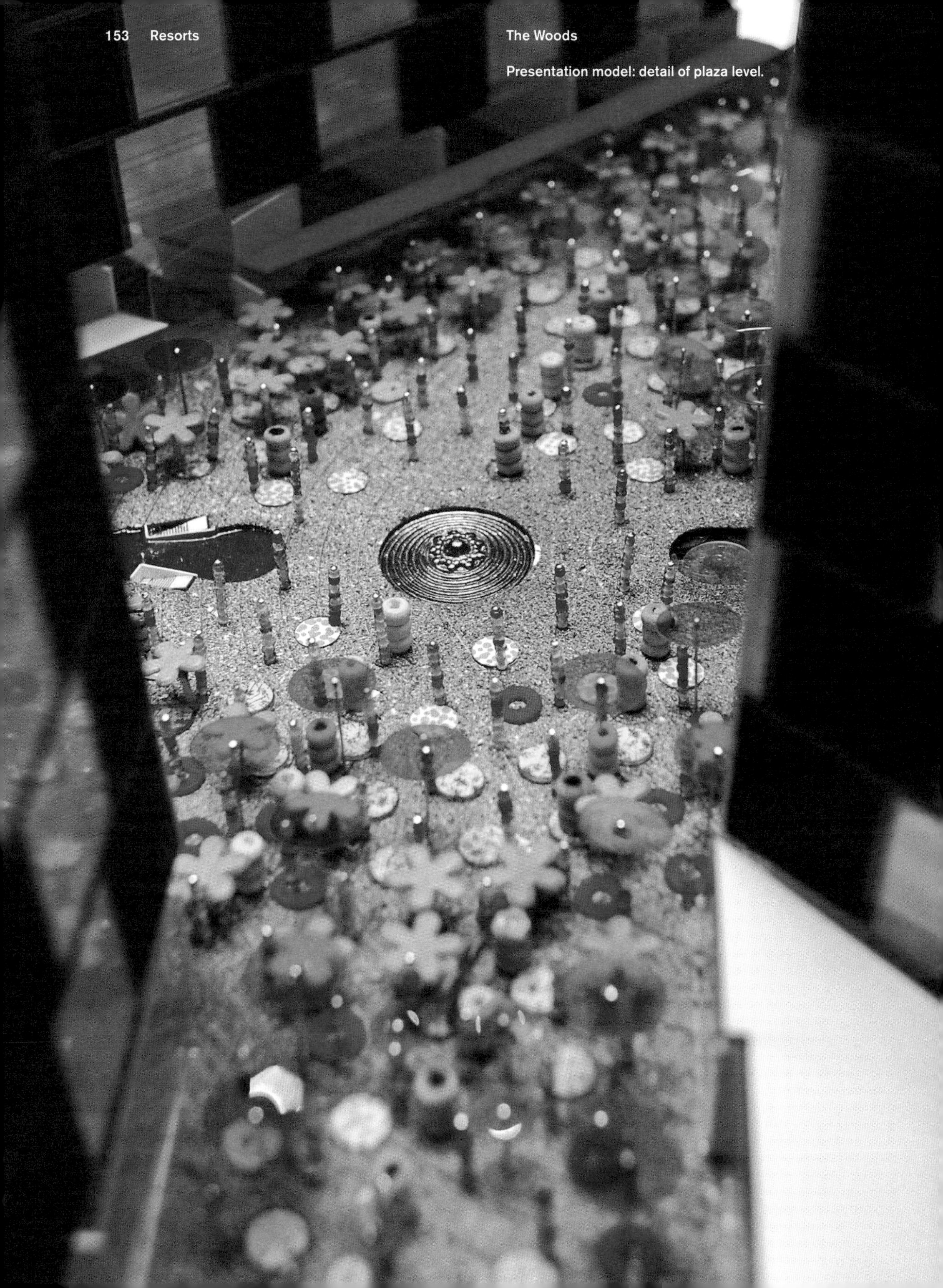

Presentation model: detail of plaza level.

The Woods

Elevations of the Woods.
Opposite top, middle and bottom: Presentation model of
hotel tower, plaza level, and casino level at grade.

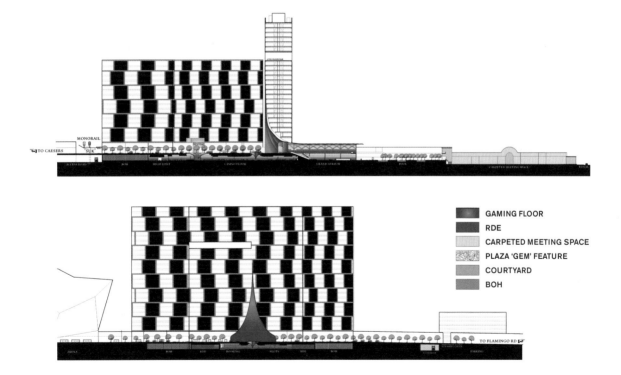

The Woods

Top: Plan of casino level at grade.
Bottom: Plan of plaza level, above grade.
Opposite: Presentation model showing view of
plaza from above.

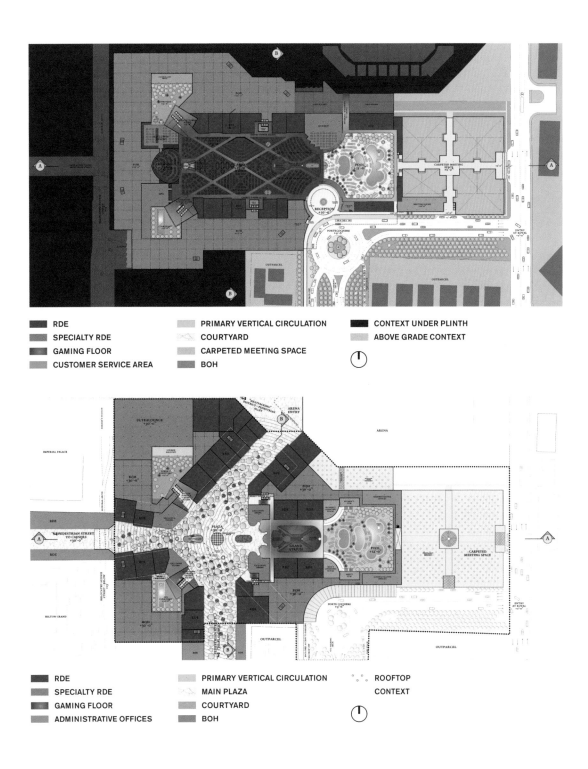

RDE
SPECIALTY RDE
GAMING FLOOR
CUSTOMER SERVICE AREA

PRIMARY VERTICAL CIRCULATION
COURTYARD
CARPETED MEETING SPACE
BOH

CONTEXT UNDER PLINTH
ABOVE GRADE CONTEXT

RDE
SPECIALTY RDE
GAMING FLOOR
ADMINISTRATIVE OFFICES

PRIMARY VERTICAL CIRCULATION
MAIN PLAZA
COURTYARD
BOH

ROOFTOP
CONTEXT

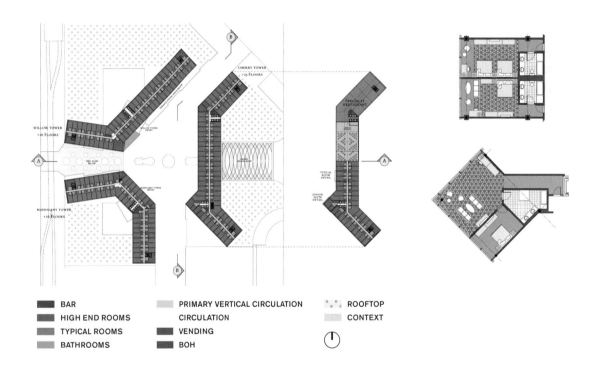

BAR

HIGH END ROOMS

TYPICAL ROOMS

BATHROOMS

PRIMARY VERTICAL CIRCULATION

CIRCULATION

VENDING

BOH

ROOFTOP

CONTEXT

The Woods

Rendering of plaza between hotel towers at night.
Opposite: Typical tower floor plan and room layout.

The Secret: Zakery Snider and Cheng-Hui Chua Twelve hundred feet from the Strip and surrounded by three parking garages, the site we selected on Harrah's campus is not at all obvious—or even desirable—for the casino's next tower. Playing up the tucked-away atmosphere of this out-of-the-way parcel, our design concept proposes a hidden world that is rich with possibilities. The tower is animated by a series of courtyards. As a branding strategy, each courtyard targets a different demographic, and the meshing of the programmatic activities surrounding the courtyards creates an unexpected sequence of events for the visitor, suggesting the surprise at the back of every secret. For example, a gaming floor may lead to an exterior pool, then to an ultra-lounge, and then to one of the courtyards. Furthermore, taking advantage of the site's less-than-suitable location, we broadened the tower's podium to allow for a medium-density structure that is low enough so that all the courtyards receive sunlight.

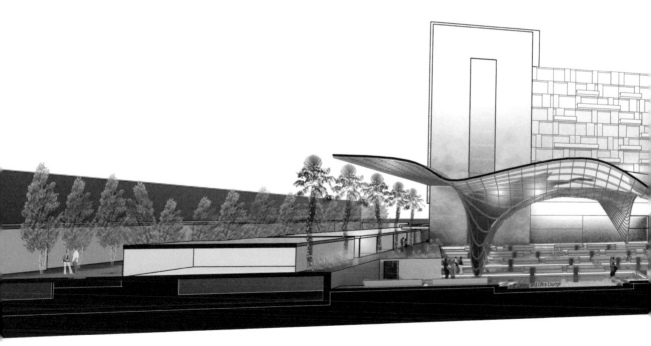

The Secret

Illustrated section through the Secret showing courtyards
and lounges.

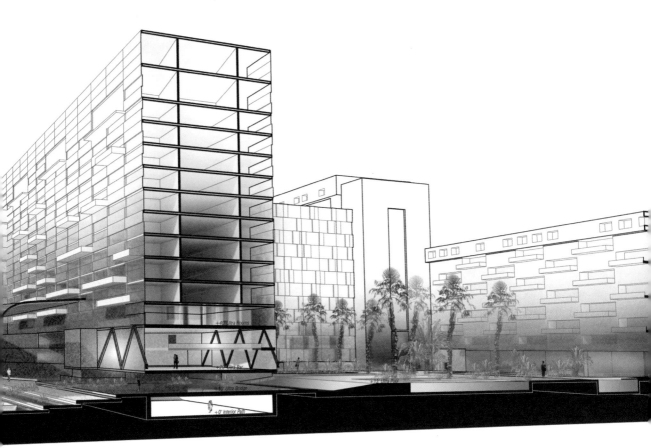

The Secret

Top: Casino entrance rendering.
Bottom: Resort entrance rendering.
Opposite: Rendering of the Secret from Koval Lane.

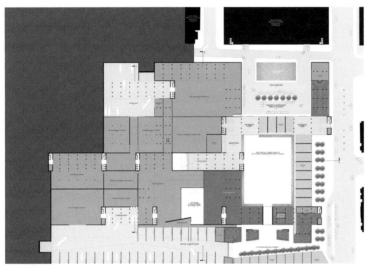

LEVEL ONE

LEVEL TWO

The Secret

Below and opposite: Plans for Koval Lane.

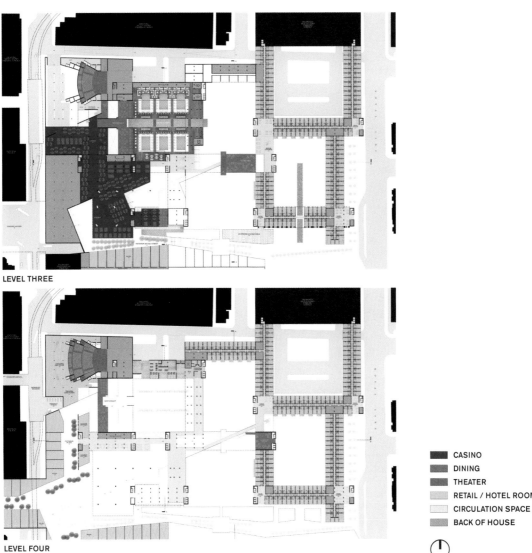

LEVEL THREE

LEVEL FOUR

CASINO
DINING
THEATER
RETAIL / HOTEL ROOMS
CIRCULATION SPACE
BACK OF HOUSE

The Secret

Ultra-lounge rendering.
Opposite: Pool and casino courtyard rendering.

Hotel V: Lauren Mishkind and Terry Chew Our design concept knits together Harrah's properties using a formal centerpiece that creates a dynamic sense of place through a variety of program. Located across from Bally's at the busy intersection of Flamingo Road and Las Vegas Boulevard, the Hotel V connects two existing pedestrian bridges to an elevated plaza, offering visitors the chance to shop, dine, or just escape the sun.

Our scheme's catch-and-sequester strategy first attracts would-be guests with a spectacular fountain, then funnels them up terraced steps to the plaza level, which connects to the main lobby of the Hotel V itself and a new pedestrian entrance to Bally's. The shaded plaza is surrounded by retail shops and—inspired by European plazas that capitalize on vistas, diversity, and foot traffic—overlooked by a terrace peppered with cafés and restaurants.

Throughout the hotel, a pinwheel strategy is used, spinning out from the elevator core each floor's corridor so that it penetrates two sides of the curtain wall. This arrangement allows natural light to brighten the hallways and registers the organization of the floor plan as it shifts to accommodate the varying program and levels of luxury. The tower's façade also acts to draw attention to specific programs, such as a restaurant, a cocktail party on a deck, the spa, the pool, and corridors.

The promotion of interaction between guests and the Strip is evident at all scales of the hotel. Within the compressed guest rooms, the bed is pushed against the window in order to create a voyeuristic opportunity; whether the curtains are drawn or open, the façade showcases the activity within. The underlying intention is to de-emphasize the physical and spatial spectacle and, instead, promote program and activity as its substitute. Hotel V serves as a framework that highlights and encases the actions, interactions, and choices of its occupants.

Hotel V

Top to bottom: Plan at ground, plaza, and terrace level.
Opposite: Hotel V outdoor plaza.

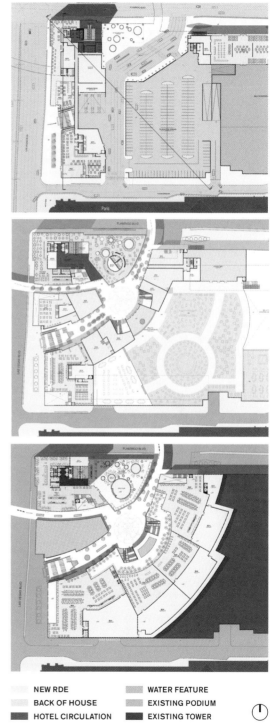

NEW RDE	WATER FEATURE
BACK OF HOUSE	EXISTING PODIUM
HOTEL CIRCULATION	EXISTING TOWER

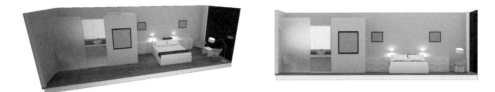

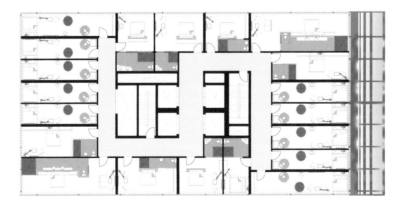

Hotel V

Hotel V outdoor plaza.
Opposite: Room types in Hotel V.

Hotel V pool deck.

The Stars: Louise Levi and Eric Krancevic Our Stars casino proposal inverts the typical Las Vegas casino organization by creating both a vibrant street fabric and a bustling pedestrian retail oasis around the resort's center, the Beach. A new kind of spectacle on the Strip, the Beach features a six-acre wading pool and provides a gradient of options for guests who are visiting the man-made oasis or staying in one of the resort's hotel rooms overlooking it. Numerous activities—an outdoor concert, a volleyball tournament, a wedding at the waterside chapel—can be programmed in this space, which hides a three-story parking garage. Sustainability is foregrounded by integrating into the project a "living machine," a site-specific filtration system that treats the water used by Harrah's properties, including a fifty-foot waterfall beneath which visitors check into their rooms. Underscored by the presence of water, the design's sustainable aspect further engages the resort's guests with a suspended orchid nursery that hangs over the LVNV nightclub's bar and anchors the resort at the street level. The suspended nursery not only allows natural lighting to penetrate the casino but also provides fresh flowers for the hotel's rooms and lounges.

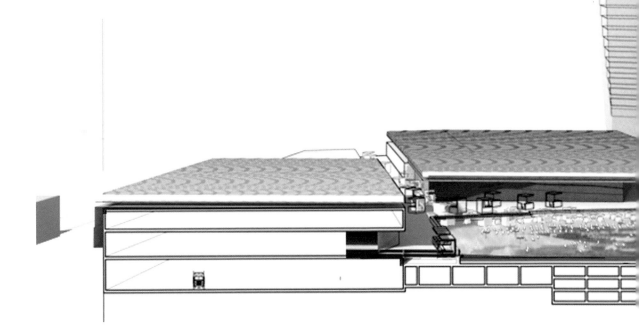

The Stars

Section showing the beach's amenity.

The Stars

Typical tower plan.
Opposite: Tower rendering from Koval Lane.

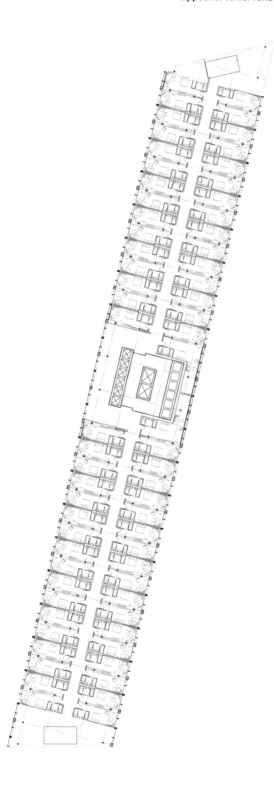

The Stars

The Stars lobby.
Opposite top: The Beach's amenity at the Stars.
Opposite bottom: Sections.

FINAL STUDIO REVIEW

From left: Robert A.M. Stern, Lauren Mishkind, Richard Fields, Sergio Kiernan, John Jacobson, Deborah Berke, Edward P. Bass, Leon Krier, David Bonderman, Elihu Ruben, and Diana Balmori.

David M. Schwarz How do you think technology will impact the next phase of Las Vegas development?

Greg Miller We need to make it real. For young people today, everything is online, from iChat to videos. Vegas is a place where you can use that technology and make it real afterward. You can overlay what is happening virtually with all the places to meet and gather.

Robert Frey What makes Las Vegas interesting is that we don't have any "cool" people. They are in New York, Miami, or Los Angeles where you can't really do anything big because the cool people move every six months. A big project in Los Angeles won't make any money, so you start a bar and make it cool for six months, then someone else can move in. In Las Vegas there is an opportunity, because there is a new customer every three days, and you can spend a lot of money to entertain them. People look forward to doing things they can't do at home. They can become a totally different person in Las Vegas than they can at home. I think when people go there, they just want to go nuts.

. . . . .

David M. Schwarz As some of the students will tell you, this semester made them look at the world differently than they've been asked to so far during their time at Yale. Why did you establish the fellowship which enabled this studio?

Edward P. Bass In architecture there are many people involved—developers who the AIA calls "owners," and the owners are, generally speaking, your clients. That is a very definite role. They are the people who need the building, and they figure out how it's going to be paid for and how it will be used. Then you have users, who are very different from the owners. The people who stay in the hotel rooms in Las Vegas are users. The people who own the restaurants, the entertainment, the lounges, and so forth are users. The people who are working for all these resorts are also users because they have functions they have to carry out as well.

This studio was set up to bring in a developer—a client—along with a master architect as a central critic with the idea that, by the time you are in your last year of architecture school, it's not a bad idea to also get exposed a little bit to how the real world of architecture works. I learned a lot about how architectural education works by going to this school and keeping up with the school. I think this is very definitely a place to challenge the architect to answer questions that normally an architect would never be asked to answer, but to use your imagination and energy to dream of things.

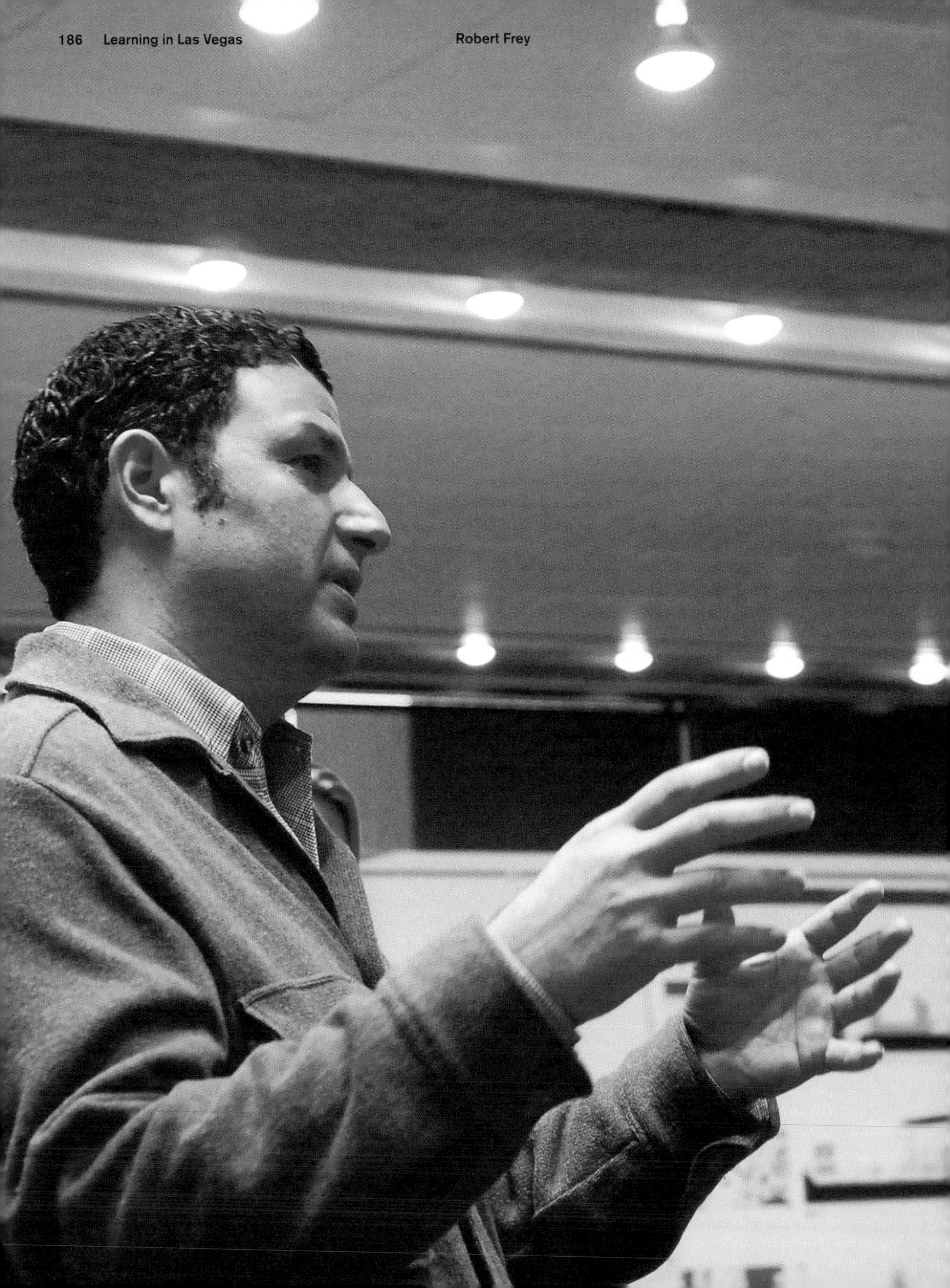

I never expected that, at a final presentation, a student, playing the role of architect, would be asked the question, what is your demographic for this hotel? Because in the real world, the architect would never be asked what is the demographic for the hotel. It starts out this way: the developer is trying to figure out the demographic and how he is going to attract that demographic and make that a profitable hotel, and the architect has to realize that for his building design. It is the developer who is going to begin with the demographic. A hotel room that is eight and a half feet wide because it is designed to be cheap just doesn't make sense, and I frankly don't see how a student would be allowed to make those decisions because those are not the architect's decisions.

A hotel developer in Las Vegas, I have great confidence, knows a lot about his particular customer and what is expected in a room, what they want in a room, and what the architect needs to design into that room—that is the real world, and that is where those decisions are made. Ultimately, the developer has to decide the budget. The architect has a vital creative role to realize something in a building that will for decades serve its purpose.

Greg Miller The architects you describe are not the architects I would hire—the architect who is just responding to a brief. I view architecture as an incredibly egotistical activity, someone—the developer, the owner, whoever—eventually has to say, "I like this." I have been in developer corporations where there is not a single entrepreneur, there is not a single decision-maker. You have a group sitting around a table, and they have a general business case, and we have tended to gravitate to architects who are prepared to mix it up and really get into trying to help forge consensus where you don't have a unitary decision-maker. Working for corporations, as opposed to working for a sovereign or working for an entrepreneur, I believe is a totally different experience.

Robert A.M. Stern That things work should be the bottom line of any enterprise, architecture or otherwise; it's the next step that separates a utilitarian approach from something greater. Clients are clients, and they'll come to you with a predetermined idea about a problem. I find, in my own experience, corporate or otherwise, that most people can be challenged in a productive way, asked to think about things in a new way. Sometimes the thinking about it in a new way does result in an actual change or refashioning of the project. Sometimes, because the client has done his or her work quite thoroughly before or there is a bottom line of economics or governmental approvals, they don't listen. Clients are creative; I think the role of being a client is as creative as the role of being an architect.

Charles Atwood I want something that, when I see it or feel it or you describe the vision of it, it is something I want to build, something that inspires me to want to do that project. Of course, I want all the requirements—the program, the economics, the planning—to be thought through and resolved in the most efficient manner. But just because that's the case doesn't mean I think it's a good project. What I look for is a vision which we can build consensus around, and to do that it needs to inspire people. For a project of this scale, we all understand that what we are looking at right now will go through many changes along the path to a building. So I'm looking for an idea that is clear and strong—so much so that it will continue to give direction over the many years it will take to develop the project.

. . . . .

David M. Schwarz One of the reasons walking down Las Vegas Boulevard is so difficult is that casino owners have, over time, made it more difficult. They've done this as a way to make it more difficult to leave their resorts. But Harrah's has acquired a number of adjacent resorts, and they find themselves in a unique situation. They can invert the old model. They can encourage people to leave one resort and walk to the next one—they'll still be in a Harrah's resort. It's an easy concept and a notion that is found all over the world. It's a neighborhood: streets, sidewalks, buildings. But you also have to remember that these buildings were not built by the same hand. They were competitors, and they all conspired to similar pedestrian-unfriendly goals. Coming in now and trying to make them friendly to pedestrians is a challenge. That was a central idea for this studio.

Greg Miller Many of these decisions have been taken out of our hands at this point because, when CityCenter opens, it will be a second-floor resort. Bellagio has a second-floor connection, and the connection we've designed at Caesars is a second-floor connection. Planet Hollywood, across the street from CityCenter, will be elevated a level above the Strip. At some point, if you believe this is the trend, you believe the pedestrians and the vehicles won't exist on the same level. That whole side of the Strip, for a mile, has already given up the sidewalk. So how does that position us? Even though the trend in Las Vegas is clear—Clark County is the biggest proponent of the grade-separated pedestrian overpasses—is this the best way forward? The intersection of the Strip and Sands Avenue, where Treasure Island is, it takes twenty minutes to cross the street to the Palazzo. You may be better off getting into a cab. I wonder if there isn't a better way for pedestrians to move around the Strip. We have around 3,000 people an hour on average moving in front of the Flamingo. But is this busier than New York City or Chicago? Pedestrians and vehicles are able to coexist on the same level in major cities throughout the world.

. . . . .

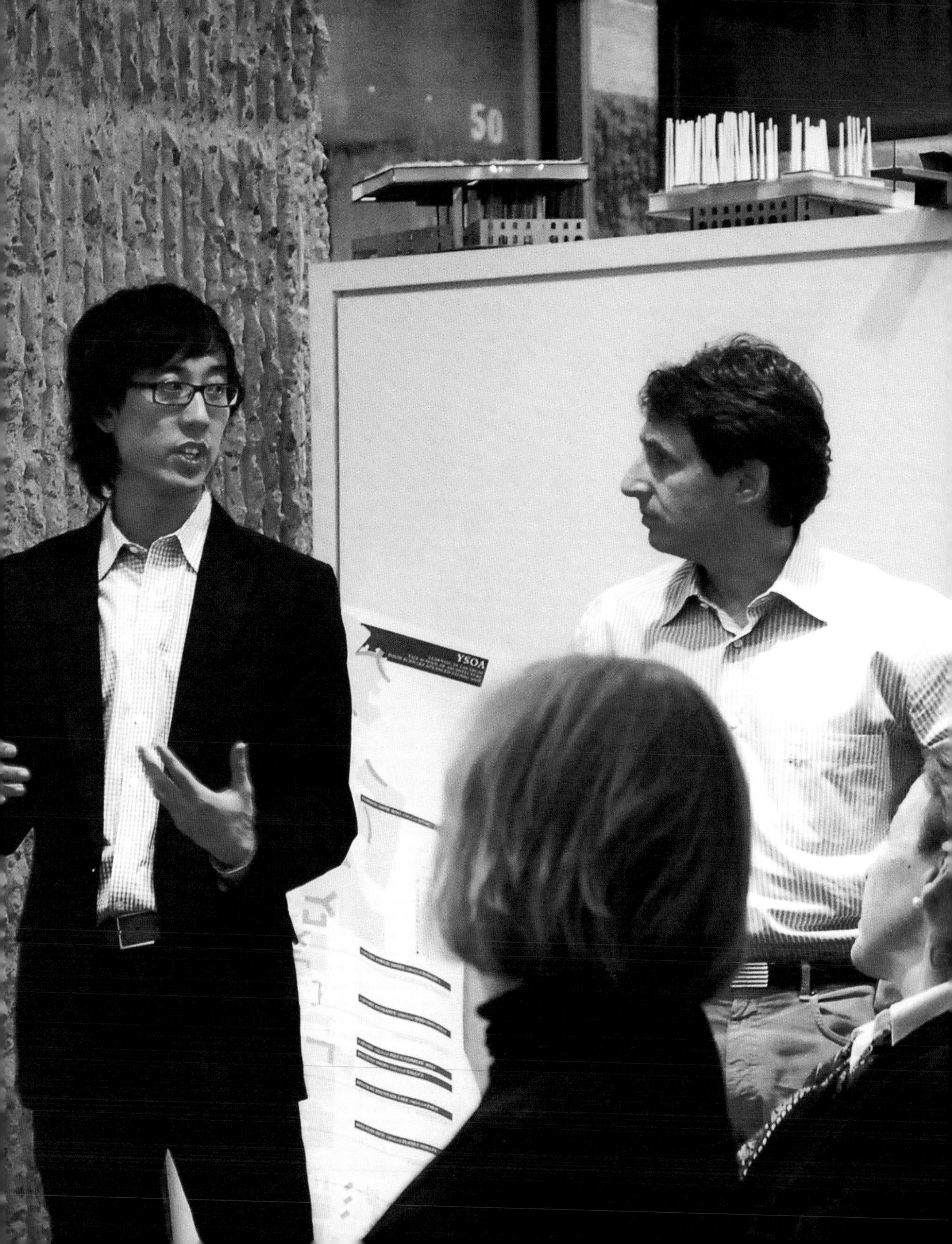

Left to right: Cheng-Hui Chua and Marc Rowan.

Edward P. Bass In many places, the model is for the casino to be at ground level; in a way, it's similar to how, in department stores, cosmetics are at the ground level. It is the most lucrative thing to draw people in; all the other activities are a level up. It is interesting to note the ways that different resorts allow the pedestrian to circulate to this second level because you still make significant income on the second level if you can get people to circulate to and through it. The best projects get people to go to both levels.

. . . . .

Charles Atwood Some buildings are not made to be porous. They were intended to make you stay. One of our ideas now is to make these buildings easier to navigate and to create more internal circulation that is friendly to pedestrians. Is there a correlation between Strip frontage of a resort and profitability? No. Some places have enormous Strip frontage, but as a result, they become isolated because they are so far away from the next place. Having the buildings close together gives you the opportunity for cross-pollination.

David M. Schwarz One of the central questions of this studio is, how do you create space of value that is not on the Strip?

David Bonderman By forcing people onto a crowded sidewalk, by having narrow spaces, you create an excitement as opposed to having broader and nicely laid out architectural spaces where you feel like you are alone. The most successful pedestrian places are the narrow sidewalks, such as those in front of the Flamingo and Margaritaville, and the least successful are those in front of MGM, where nobody bothers to walk at all. The architect complains about how the cars get too much attention and the pedestrians don't get enough, when, in fact, it's exactly the right way to do it.

Marc Rowan We wrestle with four decisions that are relevant to what you are doing. One is developing buildings versus performance or spectacle. The second is, is there a residential market? We can't figure out why we would want to live in Las Vegas. We doubt whether these massive condominium projects that are being built actually serve a purpose. I wonder how they will be doing in a few years, in ten years? The third question is, will people go outdoors? We are betwixt and between as to whether people will walk outside. If you look where the money is, the money is inside, in places like the Forum Shops, the Bellagio, Fashion Show, and the Venetian shops. Will people use something offered to them that approximates an outdoor urban experience? The last thing we wrestle with is, what is the new spectacle? What will be the new draw? Is it the London Eye? Is it the Atlanta Aquarium? These are the four things that are major issues for us in making business decisions.

When you look at business travelers, right now, Chicago is the number-one destination for business events. When you survey business travelers as to where they want to go for conventions, they want to go to Las Vegas. It is the number-one requested destination, consistently. There is no problem filling Las Vegas every Thursday, Friday, and Saturday night in any circumstance. The success we've seen as a business is Sunday through Thursday. Business travel has changed the economics. In Vegas you have ninety percent occupancy, increasing business travel and a preferred consumer destination 365 days a year. You can afford to invest here and make a real return. In places that are seasonal resorts—and we struggle with this as owners of resorts across the country—do you build a church for Easter? In Las Vegas, Easter is every day.

Greg Miller People come to Vegas and the spectacles for something they can experience here they can't experience in their normal lives. We've done a ton of research that says the reason people come is to escape. That's the reason it's popular for business travelers. No one wants to go to a regular convention hotel; you want to go to a place that has spectacle, that captures your imagination.

BIOGRA-
PHIES

Edward P. Bass has been a leader in the redevelopment of downtown Fort Worth, Texas, in what has been recognized as one of the most successful urban revitalization efforts in America. In addition to graduating from Yale College, Bass studied at the Yale School of Architecture from 1968 to 1970. He endowed the fellowship bearing his name at the School of Architecture, of which the Las Vegas studio is a beneficiary. He serves on the executive committees of the New York Botanical Garden and the Botanical Research Institute of Texas and is a founding trustee of the Philecology Trust. He is a director emeritus of the World Wildlife Fund, on whose board he served from 1988 to 2007.

David Bonderman is a founding partner of TPG Capital, which holds joint majority ownership of Harrah's Entertainment with Apollo Management LP. Prior to forming TPG in 1992, he was chief operating officer of the Robert M. Bass Group Inc. in Fort Worth, Texas. Prior to joining RMBG in 1983, he was a partner in the law firm of Arnold & Porter in Washington, D.C., where he specialized in corporate, securities, bankruptcy, and antitrust litigation. From 1969 to 1970, he was a fellow in foreign and comparative law in conjunction with Harvard University, and, from 1968 to 1969, he was special assistant to the U.S. Attorney General in the Civil Rights Division. From 1967 to 1968, he was an assistant professor at Tulane University School of Law, in New Orleans. Bonderman graduated magna cum laude from Harvard Law School in 1966.

Alan M. Feldman is senior vice president of public affairs for MGM Mirage. He is involved in a wide array of industry issues with a particular focus in areas concerning responsible gaming, serving on the boards of both the Nevada Council on Problem Gambling and the National Center for Responsible Gaming; he also previously served as a member of the Athletes and Addictions Task Force at Harvard University Medical School, Division of Addictions. He is the recipient of the 2002 Casino Management Association award for Gaming Professional of the Year. He received the Lifetime Achievement Award in Gaming Communications from the American Gaming Association in 2009.

Steven Flusty, Ph.D., is an associate professor of geography at York University, England. His primary interests are the banality of imperialisms past and present and the everyday practices of global formation, the latter a topic he interrogated most ruthlessly in *De-Coca-Colonization: Making the Globe from the Inside Out* (Routledge, 2004). His work appears in assorted electronic media and a selection of academic, professional, and popular journals.

Robert Frey is a founding partner of Pure Management Group, which owns and operates a series of nightclubs in Las Vegas and around the country. His company operates Pure nightclub in Caesars Palace, the nation's highest-grossing nightclub.

Oscar B. Goodman is the third-term mayor of the city of Las Vegas and the self-proclaimed "happiest mayor in the universe." Goodman was born and raised in Philadelphia, graduating from Haverford College and receiving his law degree from the University of Pennsylvania Law School. Prior to becoming mayor, he was named one of the "15 Best Trial Lawyers in America" by the *National Law Journal*. He also has been featured in numerous publications such as *Of Rats and Men* and even portrayed himself in the movie *Casino*. He serves on the advisory board of the U.S. Conference of Mayors.

Greg Miller is the senior vice president of resort development at Harrah's Entertainment. He is responsible for all large-scale development projects at the company, including the master-planning of Harrah's assets in Las Vegas and the development of new concepts for use both in Las Vegas and throughout the world. Previously, Miller was president of Universal Mediterranea, Universal Studio's theme-park resort in Spain. Prior to relocating to Spain, he was the senior vice president and chief financial officer of the international/new business development unit of Universal's Parks and Resorts Group. Before joining that group, Miller served in various strategic planning and finance roles at PepsiCo. Miller received a B.B.A. in 1983 from the University of Notre Dame. He later received an M.B.A., with a concentration in marketing, from the Kellogg Graduate School of Business at Northwestern University.

Pauliina Raento, Ph.D., is research director at the Finnish Foundation for Gaming Research, professor of human geography at the university in Helsinki, and associate editor of the journal *Political Geography*. Her work is mostly about politics, culture, leisure, and visual methodologies.

Marc Rowan is a founding partner of Apollo Management LP, a private investment firm that holds joint majority ownership of Harrah's Entertainment with TPG Capital. He currently serves on the board of directors of AAA and Norwegian Cruise Lines. He also serves on the boards of AP Investment Europe Ltd., BHR Holdings GP Ltd., and Apollo Principal Holdings IV GP Ltd. Prior to joining Apollo, Rowan was a member of the merger and acquisition department of Drexel Burnham Lambert Inc., with responsibilities in high-yield financing, transaction idea generation, and merger structure negotiation. Rowan graduated from the University of Pennsylvania's Wharton School of Business with a bachelor's degree and an M.B.A. in finance.

Brian Yost is the vice president of resort development at Harrah's Entertainment, where he is charged with concept and new project development. He began his professional career with Marriott Hotels and Resorts, where he rose through the ranks in restaurants, bars, and catering, ending up as director of food and beverage. He was a member of the opening team at Euro Disney and was later responsible for retail, dining, and entertainment at Walt Disney World's Pleasure Island. He returned to Marriott International, eventually becoming corporate vice president of restaurants and beverage. After the Yale studio, in 2009, Yost took a new position at Live Nation as president of amphitheaters, North American music, with responsibility for 46 amphitheaters.

Image Credits Terry Chew: 88, 89; Terry Chew, Nicholas Hanna, Lauren Mishkind and Christopher Starkey: 128–132; Terry Chew and Lauren Mishkind: 142–143, 168–175; Terry Chew and Tom Tang: 112–115; Cheng-Hui Chua: 35, 39, 43, 45, 75, 78, 81, 90–91; Cheng-Hui Chua, Nicholas Hanna and Zakery Snider: 108–111; Cheng-Hui Chua, Patrick McGowan and Zakery Snider: 124–125, 136–141; Cheng-Hui Chua and Zakery Snider: 160–167; Brook Denison: 28–31; Steven Flutsy: 56–66; Steve Hall, Hedrich/Blessing: 14, 17; Nicholas Hanna: cover, 37, 41, 47, 49, 51, 52, 73, 101; Nicholas Hanna and Christopher Starkey: 152–159; Harrah's Entertainment: 19–23, 126; Jim Hedrich, Hedrich/Blessing: 13; Eric Krancevic: 94–97; Louise Levi: 98–99, 122–123; Louise Levi and Eric Krancevic: 176–181; Louise Levi, Eric Krancevic and Christopher Starkey: 104–107; Louise Levi, Eric Krancevic and Tom Tang: 132–135; Patrick McGowan and Lauren Mishkind: 116–117; Patrick McGowan and Tom Tang: 144–151; Lauren Mishkind: 85, 86; Zakery Snider: 92–93; Christopher Starkey: 83, 84; Christopher Starkey and Tom Tang: 118–121; Tom Tang: 100; Courtesy of Venturi, Scott Brown and Associates © Philadelphia: 34, 36, 38, 40, 42, 44, 46, 48, 50; Roxane Zargham: 182–183, 185, 186, 189, 190.